To Pat,

Thank you for present & future encourag

Thank you for the opportunity to work for Ocean Bay. I am looking forward to learning a lot from you.

Much Love
&
Many Blessing

T. Ebony.

Losing Love,

Having Faith &

Finding Hope

Innerbeauty Memoirs

Terryl Ebony

Order this book online at www.trafford.com
or email orders@trafford.com

Most Trafford titles are also available at major online book retailers.

Printed in the United States of America.

ISBN: 978-1-4669-4769-6 (sc)
ISBN: 978-1-4669-4768-9 (hc)
ISBN: 978-1-4669-4770-2 (e)

Library of Congress Control Number: 2012913458

Trafford rev. 03/05/2013

 www.trafford.com

North America & international
toll-free: 1 888 232 4444 (USA & Canada)
phone: 250 383 6864 ♦ fax: 812 355 4082

True Beauty Comes from within

"Faith is no irresponsible shot in the dark. It is a responsible trust in God, who knows the desires of your hearts, the dreams you are given, and the goals you have set. He will guide your paths right."

—Robert Schuller—

Dedication

The first selection of my memoirs is dedicated to my son.

I love you so much. You are my reason for living. You are my heart, my soul and my inspiration. Even in my bleakest moments, know that I am working with you and praying for you to find the peace, strength and happiness you deserve. I pray you take from me whatever energy you need to overcome the obstacles life will throw your way. I have watched you grow into a handsome, bright, and opinionated young man. Take that with you throughout life as you transform into the man that God has intended. You were predestined for greatness. I know you will touch many lives with your performing gifts. Son, I am very proud of you. Always walk in God's light and know that your dreams are just a step away from reality. You just have to believe they are attainable. I love you.

Contents

Acknowledgments

I want to acknowledge those people who have played a critical part in a chapter of my life called—*Losing Love, Having Faith & Finding Hope . . .*

To my Lord and Savior, Jesus Christ. I thank you for always watching over me and giving me the strength and guidance to continue even when I feel like giving up. There were times when I did not tap into your many blessings and you still loved me. I thank you for providing me with a small yet powerful support team. Although I did not understand then, I do now. Trials and tribulations are only stumbling blocks that lead to ultimate success—which is not defined by dollars but by the love that surrounds me and the love that I am able to give back in return.

To my mother, Monica Pickering. Thank you! Thank you for being such a wonderful human being and a loving mom. Through your eyes and loving arms, I learned how to selflessly love my child as well as others. I learned the payoff of hard work and sacrifice. I do not know where I would be today without you by my side. I know that I did not always make it easy for you and for that I apologize. Know that I treasure you and I love you immensely.

To the rest of my family—With a special acknowledgment to Marlon, Kayla, Pauline, Tricia, and Alfred.

Marlon—you were there for both my son and me from the wonder years to present. You were my anchor when I felt my ship sinking and gave me hope when I felt hopeless. I believe that God gives us all a partner and someone strong to stand beside us; I do not think it was coincidental that we fell in love, but part of the grand design called destiny. I am thankful to have you in my life.

Kayla—you are a new addition to my life and family. You have already taught me so much about forgiveness, love, inner-strength, and most importantly, you have taught me about myself. Funny thing is that you have done all that without saying a word, just being who you are and present in my life. I love you very much. You will forever be my Pumpkin Pie.

Pauline—I have never really viewed you as my aunt, but more as my big sister. Your door is always open. Your shoulders are always available without judgment. You are a true prize and demonstrate the real meaning of "unconditional love." I thank you for always being there for me even when you did not agree.

Tricia—You are my only sister and I love how our relationship evolves with time. I see the differences and similarities in people although they are cut from the same branch. I admire the fact that you do not allow others to dictate your actions. You have a mind of your own and you follow your instincts. I love you.

Alfred—you came into my life at a time when I thought father figures were just words. You showed me that you had enough love in your heart for not only my mother but her children and her children's children. The gratitude I feel is more than words can say.

To my inspirational family—Onika Pascal, Ival, Judith, Lisa, The Hewitt Family, and Kathy.

Pascalle, I would not be the person I am today nor would have been inspired to write this book if I had not met you. You are truly an inspiration. You are also a go-getter and we have so much in common. Thank you for being so open about life and your beliefs.

Ival - my sister from another mother –Thank you for being my voice of reason. You keep me grounded at times when I think I am invincible and bite off more than I can chew.

Judith—You challenge my thoughts and make me reach deep inside which ultimately gives me added strength and reassurance in the decisions I make. Lisa—I do not know where to begin to express the gratitude for your presence in my son's life. A great deal of the person he is growing up to become is attributed to the time, wisdom and love that you have bestowed upon him over the years. For that, I am eternally grateful. To the Hewitt Family (especially Neil and Michelle)—my life savers. When I was at my darkest point, you scooped me up, took me in, and made me a part of your family. You made me feel safe and gave me reasons to smile, to eat, and to believe in a brighter tomorrow. I owe you and my son owes you. And, Kathy—my spiritual sister. You were there when my judgment was clouded by tribulation, always reminding me to trust and have faith in God, especially in times of despair.

I hold each of you near and dear to my heart, and I want to extend my deepest and sincerest gratitude and thanks to you all. I love you so much.

A special thank you also goes to all the people who offered their thoughts and reassurances on the growing problem of parent-child conflicts. I hope your words will touch and encourage someone. I would like to thank my editors—Shonell

Bacon, Linda Colbert-Chenet, and Elizabeth Parke. I would also like to thank all those who encouraged and supported me as I was writing this book. I believe that everyone comes into our lives for a reason and serves a purpose or teaches a lesson. So to everyone else I have had the pleasure of crossing paths with, I thank you too and wish you many blessings.

Thank you
and
God Bless

Introduction

In life, we go through many trials and tribulations. I decided to share with you some of the significant things I have experienced. I do not regret having faced many of these obstacles because overcoming them is what contributed to the development of the "me" I am today. Jumping each hurdle gave me the confidence to withstand the next. It was not easy and many were not pleasant, but I made it and eventually the good outweighed the bad. Every day is a struggle but with prayer and lots of faith, I make it through and so can you.

This book is written not only to tell a story, but also to show the errors and the triumphs of being a single parent. I offer advice *(in the italicized paragraphs)* as a Mother, Life Skills/Parent Coach, Producer and Host of an online parenting radio show, and Founder/Executive Director of a non-profit organization whose mission is to help understand, develop and stimulate the minds of our youth. I have been there and done that. My goal is for others to learn and better their journey!

"Losing Love, Having Faith & Finding Hope"

- -

It is, in retrospect, one of the hardest events a parent can go through. This is a story of the importance of parenthood and childhood, especially that of a boy needing his father—despite—having his mother. This situation is all too common, but no one seems to really understand the effects it has on all parties involved—mother, father and child. Well, I have experienced it first hand and tried to pay attention to all the key players and their roles and responsibilities. Too many of us talk about our neighbor, friend, or family member and the way they treat their children or manage their homes. We are often so busy investigating and gossiping about someone else's life that we tend to overlook what is going on in our own backyard. Then before you know it, our homes are in total chaos and we have no clue how it got that way, much less how to fix it.

Losing Love, Having Faith & Finding Hope is about three main characters: Love—the father, Faith—the mother and Hope—their son. Their story will touch you and make you think about the relationship with your spouse or partner. Is it worth keeping or would it be healthier to walk away? You will also think about the relationship with your child or the role you may play in a child's life. What can you do to strengthen that relationship or develop it if it does not exist? You will see how significant your role is as a parent and how easily things can—and will—spiral out of control if constant positive communication is not present. This book will show you, as a parent, harsh realities concerning the consequences of *your* actions. It will hopefully empower you to take responsibility for your decisions (whether good or bad) regardless of the outcome and own it. My hope is that if you can see yourself somewhere in this book, you will then take the necessary steps to begin changing your behavior and thought process.

My sincere intent is to open the eyes and minds of men and women *before* they become parents. I want to give personal and logical insight as to what it takes to be a good parent. Hopefully, my story will be an inspiration, as well as, a guide for the highs and lows that will occur. Now, not everyone will go through the same things but the basics are the basics. And, for those of you who are already parents, I hope that you will think about the relationship you have with your children and determine if everything possible is being done to provide for them physically, mentally, spiritually, emotionally and financially. Remember, quite often, emotional wounds cut far deeper than physical ones. My prayer is that my experiences and lessons learned will lead to better parenting and a healthier family lifestyle. Use my story as a big mirror to see how you handle personal and parental situations. I want you to see how those decisions can affect your child, especially when parents are in conflict, or when one parent is absent from the home.

Before you embark on the crucial, life-altering journey of parenthood, know that, critical decisions—must be made. Decide if you "really" know yourself and what YOU want out of life (not your parents, your boyfriend, your girlfriend, family member or teacher). You must be certain of you! Decide whether you are ready to handle the total responsibility that comes with the conception of human life. Decide what, if any, sacrifices you are willing to make to put the life that you create at the center of your masterpiece (masterpiece being your life). Decide if you are capable of wrapping your mind around unconditional love. Most people cannot, but when you have a child, you must. Loving a child requires that you give almost as much as you would give yourself and sometimes more. Most people cannot accept the fact that mankind fails us more often than not. A child is human and will err; will disappoint; will fall short—but this does not mean you give up. Once you are a parent, you cannot give your child back. You cannot neglect your fiscal, emotional or physical responsibility. Becoming a parent is the single most important undertaking in ones' life. Therefore, it should receive the maximum amount of consideration prior to the decision of conception.

Having a child evokes unconditional love. It just happens! Unconditional love does not mean condoning wrong doings or spoiling your child. It *does* mean maintaining love *despite* the wrong doing as well as good deeds. Most of the time, when we as parents try to understand the characteristics of our child's negative behavior, we tend to look at the surface issues and draw conclusions based on that. However, surface situations are usually a collection of bigger problems stemming from past experiences with us—the parent(s)—not the child. Your child's actions are often the *reaction* of some underlying situation that has occurred at home, in school, with their peers, etc., we as parents are unaware of or often ignore. This is why being open-minded and not judgmental is very critical. Wouldn't it be sad to judge your child and later find that you had a significant role in his/her dysfunctional behavior? Think about it! The other consideration is that when we do come to the realization that we are partially to blame, we *seldom own* that responsibility much less apologize for it. If we expect a child to own his/her mistakes, then we as adults and parents must do the same.

It has been my experience that many parents fail to share any responsibility in their child's downturns. They are only there to reap the praises when the child is doing well or when there is something positive to report. So what does this teach your child? "It is ok to run away from mistakes and not take responsibility for negative actions? You only have to own up to the good things you do and not the bad?" Is that the proper lesson you really want to teach your child? I highly doubt it. The reality is, we do it almost every day without realization. But, is that being a good and responsible parent? Good parents take responsibility for their good and bad choices and teach their child to do the same. When your child witnesses you taking responsibility for your negative actions or decisions, it shows them that *you too* are human and will make mistakes. It lets them see that it is okay to make a mistake and it is okay to tell the truth even if it results in negative consequences. If you want your child to take ownership of his or her actions, then you as the parent must set that example. Practice what you preach!

A child's actions may be his own, but the reason behind those actions *usually* belongs to someone else. Find the reason behind the action and you just may be able to stop the action from reoccurring. Good parenting is not making excuses for your child. Good parenting is not rewarding your child for bad behavior. Good parenting is not always giving into your child or doing what the child wants. A good parent knows and creates boundaries; knows when to say no, even though, the "no" may mean tears and disappointment. Good parenting is not just about nice clothes, fancy restaurants, family trips, and things of that nature. Good parenting is the positive dialogue between you and your child; the positive images that you put in your child's mind; the interest that you show in the things that interest them; and the love and attention you give when you are completely exhausted and want your personal space. Those are things that your child will remember and duplicate when the time comes for them to be parents.

There is no perfect science to parenting. You may be a good mother or a good father and your child may *still grow up* with issues. We all have issues. However, you will have to find solace knowing that you did your best and gave it your all. So, if nothing else is absorbed through this reading, I hope you will examine the relationship you have with your child and strengthen it and/or find ways to make a positive difference in another child's life. They need you. They depend on you. If you let them down now, it should not come as a big surprise if they let you down later. After all, they learn from the best—*YOU!*

Real Love

Can you tell when your love is real?
Love is real when you have trust
Trust is real when you are honest with one another
Honesty comes through communication with each other

Without these things your love is not real
Without these things love cannot be sealed
Trust is something that takes time to earn
Trust is something that some people learn

Honesty should be there starting from day one
Honesty should be there from day start to day done
If you have this honesty and trust
You will know what you are feeling is love and not lust.

—Terryl Ebony

CHAPTER 1:
Humble Beginnings

A Vision of Love and the Affection of Faith

They say opposites attract. How true that is in this case, because there were definitely no similarities. Yet still, a meeting of the minds—led to a meeting of the eyes—which—led to a meeting of a more intimate side. It took a while before the union commenced. Growing up on the same block, there were years where they did not get along. They barely exchanged pleasantries if they crossed paths. Then, there was high school. The two rode the bus and train every morning, along with other friends from around the way. Eventually they began to speak, got to know each other from a teenage perspective: love, laughter, tears, funny jokes and unleashed fears. They realized there was something there between them—something they never expected—a friendship. This new found friendship grew with every passing day. After a while, they had to admit their relationship had reached another turning point. This friendship had turned into a deeper like—and then—an even deeper love. They decided to see where and how far it would go. So, when the day came for the two to join as one, it was as if time stood still in a faithful moment of loving silence—to watch the unification of two souls as they consummated ***A Faithful Love.***

Walking hand in hand, they were like two peas in a pod. Where you saw one you saw the other. They were inseparable. There was no doubt, love was in the air. Everything seemed perfect. Nothing was too much for them to handle. All the nay-sayers stood in awe and disbelief as these two opposites—not only came together in harmony—but they were actually happy! They knew what they felt, followed their hearts, ignored all the negativity and focused on their growing love. This was their way of life for a little over a year. Then eyes wondered and tempers flared. Who said teenage love was easy? Who said any love was easy?

Their love was eminent, but Faith wanted more. She expected something from Love that he was not able to provide—monogamy. Although Faith was filled with heartache and heartbreak she still held on to Love; but Love could not resist the enticement of other women. This would lead to their demise. He was torn for a while. He tried to remain faithful, but the voices of friends, family and his growing loins were the driving force of his decision. The pull was too strong. He could not resist temptation. Faith tried and seriously thought their love would be enough to sustain the aftermath of his betrayal. She was right, but she was wrong!

Although Love found himself attracted to other people, there was still a part of him that lusted and loved what Faith had to offer. There was something about her that he could not walk away from. She, too, had an undeniable fixation on him. She was constantly drawn back by his words, his dimples and his touch. But most of all she was drawn to the way he made her feel when they were together. Maybe Faith's inexperience and naiveté made her think one magical moment would change Love's way of thinking. Maybe sex could be exchanged for one's heart, love and compassion? Faith liked how she felt when she was with him and she realized she would have to work twice as hard if she did not want to lose it. She would not give up that easily. She felt that she could change him, make him forget about the other women and focus only what the two of them shared.

What was she thinking? You cannot change people. It is not a part of our human make-up to change people. People can and will only change who they are if that is their desire. And for some people that may take longer than others. For some it may never occur at all. That is the truth of the matter.

You have to acknowledge to yourself that there is something you are lacking or unhappy with in order for real change to begin. If you believe that you are content and not making wrong decisions, then why would you want to change? In fact, it can become very frustrating when someone else is constantly telling you that you should change this or that about yourself. Imagine being around someone who is always trying to "fix you" when you clearly do not see a problem. This causes a lot of conflict in most relationships. However, just because you do not notice the issue, does not mean it does not exist. It also does not mean it does.

*Both parties have to have an open mind about how the other is thinking and communicating a concern. It is all in the delivery! If I tell you **I think** or **I want** you to change something about yourself, you will more than likely shut down or become defensive. However, **if I show you** what I think is wrong, you will be more open to conversation and it can possibly result in a positive change. Effective communication is key and that is what both Faith and Love lacked.*

For years, there was a constant struggle to make their relationship work. One month they would break up and the next month they would make up, enough to make you dizzy. You were not sure what to expect from these two from one day to the next. Everyone was confused but for whatever reason, the couple knew they were not ready to say goodbye. Not yet—and—not for quite some time.

Another year had gone by with the same back and forth. Love was living his life with the luxury of having his cake and eating it too. Faith settled for the contentment of the "what if" syndrome. "What if" we can make things work? "What if" I did things differently? "What if" things could be the way they used to be? Faith was still living in the past. In her mind, she kept going back to those days when they used to have fun in the sun and enjoyed life in the moment. To her, those moments meant everything! It brought out the good 'ole days and created dreams of a hopeful future. Faith held on to that feeling and those memories for dear life and hoped Love would, too. Still, nothing changed. Everything remained as it was until that day when Faith got served an unexpected curve ball called Life—a new life that is! What would she do now? What did this all mean? Nineteen and pregnant, surrounded by doubts and a relationship built on "what ifs". This could not be good. This could not be happening. This was not a part of the plan!

Faith thought long and hard before sharing her news because she was uncertain of his reaction. After all, she was still processing all of this herself. What would this mean for her life now? What it mean for their future? With mixed emotions, Faith knew she had to say something sooner rather than later. She could not and would not keep such a secret for too long.

When she finally decided to break the news to Love, there was that initial shock. Then, there was the surreal moment of happiness to becoming a father and starting a family. Quickly, the shock wore off and happiness turned into fear, uncertainty and denial. Faith was undoubtedly hurt by Love's reaction, but knew she had to live with his decision. But, how?

Shortly thereafter, everyone would know that parentage was near for these two. All the commentators, the well-wishers, and the haters came out to give their opinion. The most popular comment or question was, "Did she get pregnant purposefully, so she could trap Love in a relationship?" Faith was amused by the skeptics but offended that Love was actually entertaining the comments, especially when you consider the fact that it takes two people to conceive a child. It was also up to both of them to use protection and knowingly, neither of them did for many years. So it really should not have come as a surprise to Love that, eventually, pregnancy and parenthood would be a strong possibility. Unfortunately, that did not happen. Love did not know how to deal with everything: Faith—and the prospect of becoming a father. So, he chose to ignore it—and her.

When people are faced with opposition, they can handle it in one of three ways. They can face the reality—head on—ignore it, or choose to remain in denial. Facing the reality puts you in a better position to have more positive results. Ignoring the reality will only prolong the inevitable, thus giving you immediate, yet inconclusive results of the inevitable. You can run but you cannot hide. And lastly, denying the reality will only hurt all concerned including you. It is the coward's way out and will only give you negative results when it's all said and done.

Ignorance is unknown and denial is refusal. Both choices yield negative results. Do not compromise your integrity; that will never be good for you on any level.

For Love, coming from a world where everything was handed to him on a silver platter, having a baby and having to share his life would definitely be a new experience. He would now have to do the giving. Was he ready for such a sacrifice at 20 years old? Was he ready to commit totally to someone other than himself? He knew he was not ready or able so he was against the idea of bringing a new life into the world at that time. But Faith could not bear the thought of terminating her pregnancy.

She held steadfast to the roller coaster she was about to embark on. She knew she was not prepared for what was to come, nor could she anticipate the future. It would be hard, but she was strong and faith that she could handle anything she put her mind to. Faith stayed true to her word, true to her heart, and true to the thought of holding her newborn child.

The next nine months were going to be very emotional and Faith had to get through it. If things were not complicated enough, Faith was laid off from her job around the same time she found out she was pregnant. After living on her own for the last year and a half, she made the decision to move back to her mother's house to have her child.

Depression and suppression took over. Love had moved on without second thoughts or feelings for what Faith was enduring. Meanwhile, as anger filled her mind, love filled her heart and Hope filled her belly. Psychologically, a compilation of emotions engulfed Faith—an inability to wrap her psyche around her current situation, lack of maturity, lack of wisdom, lack of experience and the lack of support from the love she claimed her own.

One cannot genuinely commit to someone else if they have not yet made commitments to themselves. It is hard to make others happy if you yourself are not happy. These are little things that couples should think about prior to having unprotected sex, conceiving a child, or deciding to become parents. Once that child is conceived your future, your dreams, your needs and your desires are no longer your own. It becomes shared with your unborn. Every decision and action from that point forward must take into consideration the life which the mother holds inside her womb—waiting to be born. Then once the child is born, the responsibility only intensifies and becomes more.

At this point, Love had his eyes and his mind set on someone else. There was no room in his life for either Faith or Hope. However, at times, there were flickers of sensitivity that pierced through faithful eyes with confidence and belief that all would be fine and return to normal—a time when they only had eyes for each other. Love would rub her belly and try to comfort her with words of encouragement. He had a dimpled smile and brown eyes that would shine, giving optimism that he was happy and awaiting the big day. Faith, still in denial, viewed those smiles as hope that there was still a chance they could be a family and raise their unborn child together.

Reality came quickly, and quite harshly as Faith attended prenatal visits and sonogram viewings without him by her side—experiencing heartburn—with no one to buy her vanilla ice-cream. She felt the stretching and kicking inside with no one to soothe the uncomfortable feeling or share in the wonders of the new life she had growing inside her. There were times when Love would make excuses as to why he was not there and other times when he was blatantly honest. He wanted nothing to do with Faith and being that she decided not to terminate the pregnancy, he would only perform his fatherly duties after the child was born. He had no real intention to make a commitment to her. Faith began to face that harsh reality and struggled with the idea of raising a child on her own—not because of her own insecurities—but because of her thoughts of Hope—her unborn.

Faith and Love would argue frequently. Faith was visibly and verbally irate. There was no compromise, no medium ground, and no neutral place to call a truce. She was confused by all the mixed signals and dimpled smiles. What was real and what was not? All she knew was she was pregnant, alone and tired of looking at this man parade up and down enjoying his life while she was stuck in this unattractive, swollen body.

Faith had no idea what the future held for her and her baby. She was still young, inexperienced, and growing increasingly apprehensive about her future. She continued to give the benefit of doubt to the one that helped to create the life she held inside. She still had hopes of living the all American dream—the picture perfect family—with two parents, the kids, the dog and the white picket fence. Unfortunately, her dreams were far-fetched from reality.

Faith began to rely on others to help her through this tough time. She did not want to eat. It hurt to digest. She did not want to talk. It even hurt to think. She did not want to sleep. The nightmares were too painful. She just laid there—tissue in hand—crying her sorrows away. Friends and family would have to be her strength. She was crippled with grief and filled with uncontrollable rage. She could not be reasonable or produce a rational thought. There was just hurt that came from the heart and told a painful story on her face.

Her friends tried to nourish her body and her mind with food and laughter, anything that would not remind her of her current woes. They reminded her that she was not alone. She had support even if it was not from the one who truly mattered to her. They also reminded her that every decision she made going forward affected not only her but the one she held nearest and dearest to her—her soon to be born child. So with all faith in hand, she began to smile; she began eat; she began to nourish her body and her soul—with a new mindset—of hopeful beginnings. It was then that she started to look at life from not only her eyes, but also through the eyes of her unborn child.

- -

What emotional damage was being done to the fetus, while drawing breath and feeding off of every emotional and nutritional crumb that she consumed (or did not)? Pregnant mothers not only need to consider the food they eat, but the food they do not eat and how that will affect their child. You must think about your emotional state—at all times—because children can take on the emotions of their mother from inside the womb which may dictate many of their future characteristics. From inside the womb, children are influenced by the tones of your voice and those surrounding you; they also pick up on your emotions. They may not know why the feeling occurred, but they do know there was some type of feeling involved: love, hate, joy, pain, laughter, or sadness. Many times we wonder why a child is so angry or so happy. Think back to when you were carrying them inside you, what were your overall feelings and emotions on a daily basis? The answers that you seek may lie in that discovery alone. Remember, emotional energy is transferable (good or bad), even within the womb.

- -

The ultimate measure of a man is not where he stands in moments of comfort and convenience, but where he stands in times of challenge and controversy."

—Dr. Martin Luther King, Jr.—

Inside Mother's Womb

From the time of conception inside mother's womb
Her body changes and her hormones rage
Preparing for a child to bloom

Of the life altering times ahead
Body shapes and emotions soar
Sonograms to see the core

Of the stage you have set
And there is no looking back
No matter your flaws or what you lack

There is someone now depending on you
To give them hope and see them through
From inside Mother's womb

Do not take for granted what your eyes cannot see
Inside Mother's womb
Holds life's most precious treat

40 weeks gone by—in a womb without sight
He is used to his safe haven
Imagine his fright

It is time to break free and assume your rightful place
And do great things as a prince with a silver spoon
And to think . . .

It all started inside Mother's womb

—*Terryl Ebony*

CHAPTER 2:
New Life

He was conceived: one moment, one sperm, one egg and one night of passion. One night of consummated love led to years of Hope lost in Love.

Conceived from love, torn apart at conception—from the start you feel the deception. Where once there was love and unity, now lays distrust and speculation. Knowing what was to come and not being able to deal with the reality, we run in defense. The walls go up.

- -

Some women put up a wall and a sign that says, "I am invincible. I do not need help to conquer all the trials and tribulations to come." This has become the norm for some women to try and convince a man they are strong. We try to take on the world and in most cases we usually succeed. However, if there is a child involved, it is usually the child who suffers in the long run. A child needs both parents or at least a male and female figure to admire and respect. Contributions are made from each side—both from father and mother. Women must learn to understand and accept that fact. Men must learn and accept they cannot run away from the responsibility of fatherhood and leave the burden on the mother to try and accomplish their job—or leave a child—to figure out this complicated thing called life, without a father's guidance. That would be setting both mother and child up for failure. This also applies to those mothers who have decided to abandon their kids and leave the sole responsibility to the fathers. Both parents have an obligation to their child(ren) and can provide something unique and positive if they do not realize their value in a child's life.

Some men put up a wall and a sign that says, "I am not ready to take on such responsibility." Some would argue that they are not ready, or that they are uncertain, overwhelmed and frightened. Many women experience this also but at a lesser level. Many times it would help if the father knew that the mother was feeling an equal sense of apprehension. If they tried, they could work through their fears together. But instead, because of the lack of communication, the mother tends to cover up her true feelings in order to hide her vulnerability and appear strong and independent. The man tends to go into a state of denial. They continue to live their lives as though the next nine months, nine years or the rest of their lives for that matter will not be altered. That denial in the beginning usually transforms into their reality, taking away their sense of responsibility. Again, the child is the one who suffers in the long run and the responsibility will still be there.

- -

Both walls are made of brick. Both heads are made of unbendable steel. But, the fact still remained; everyday, life was growing. Everyday set the tone for what would happen next. Everyday a child's life depended on two people who cared for each another but did not know how to show it or communicate it, two people who had different views of their future and two people who could not stay in the same room with each other long enough to make positive, informed decisions—concerning the future of their child.

At this point, Faith was at the height of her pregnancy—things between her and Love had not improved. Faith tried to keep busy, thinking of ways she could make a decent life for her and her baby with or without Love. Of course she wanted him there, and she left the door open for his return, not realizing the eminent hurt she was causing herself and her baby. She needed to start living for herself and the growing life inside of her. Depression and self-pity were no longer an option. Hopeful movements and hopeful kicks is what saved Faith from mental destruction. She knew then, that in the end it would be all worthwhile. So she continued talking, singing songs, and leaning on friends and family for strength and courage until the day her child was ready to come into the world.

When that night came and Faith began to feel discomfort, it was time for her baby to finally grace the world with his hopeful presence. She did not think twice about calling Love to tell him the much anticipated news. He came; she showered; and they left. They took a cab to the hospital where they were told that she was having contractions but not dilated enough to be in labor. They were instructed to go back home and have Faith do a lot of walking and come back in a few hours if the pain intensified. It was 12am; nervous that she would have her baby in the back seat of a cab, Faith refused to leave. Instead, she decided that she would just walk around the hospital. So, the two walked up and down the hospital stairs and around the cafeteria for hours. Eventually, Faith's mother left her job to join them at the hospital. They would all wait and walk together. Faith would start of walking at a slow moderate pace, but as the pain increased, so did her speed. She would take off—almost running—as if this would ease her pain.

At 5am, Faith could not endure the pain of the contractions any longer. Screaming and crying, she begged her mother and Love to find out if she could be examined again. She believed she was definitely in labor. The doctors determined that she was dilated 5cm but to deliver the baby you needed to be 10cm. However, they said at 5cm, they could at least admit her and give her a room. This made her a little more comfortable. They offered her a shower which was like music to her ears. The warm water beating down on her belly was soothing—more to her anxiety than to the pain. At one point, Love was near by the shower room when Faith cried out for pain. Love peaked in to make sure everything was alright. Scared and in excruciating pain, Faith grabbed Loved and pulled him into the shower—fully clothed. She just needed someone to hold on to as she went through the contractions. When she got out shower, she was introduced to her mid-wives that would help her bring her baby into the world. It was 7am; they re-examined her and told her it was time to deliver her baby.

It was hard and stressful but worth every scream and pain. With Love on one side, her mother on the other, and her midwives at her feet, Faith could ask for nothing more. She had the perfect team at her side, through every scream and every push. This was her first time experiencing such pain and anguish. She was very nervous that something would go wrong. She kept checking in with her mid-wives to make sure everything was going according to plan. Every time she was told to push, she would push and squeeze Love and her mother's hands. At 11:06am on 11/11/94, Hope was born. An exhausted Faith just wanted to hold her son, before falling to sleep.

For the first time, Faith had both Love and Hope. In her eyes, everything was as it should be. She now had two men to make her heart skip a beat. Hope was perfect, a ray of sunshine. This was the best thing that ever happened to Faith and maybe the worst thing that ever happened to Love. He just was not ready . . . .

When Faith woke up, reality began to set in—Love and Faith were parents! They had a child to care for, to feed, to clothe, to educate, and to support. Everyone was happy at the joy Hope brought to their lives. He already stamped his permanent mark into their hearts and souls. Faith could not help but wonder if this would make a difference. Would this now make them a family and fulfill her dream? No such luck. Love maintained his own thoughts of co-parenting. There was no sign of him giving up his current lifestyle of no ties, no commitments, and no responsibilities. And, although it was said and evident throughout the duration of her pregnancy, Faith still held on to that glimmer of light that she saw in Love's eyes every now and again.

Faith was hit with reality later on that day as she laid in her hospital bed and visitors came to share in her joy. When she opened her eyes, she wondered, "Who was this strange face looking down at me with an uncertain smile?" What a way to meet your replacement! "The timing could not be more perfect", she thought with a smile to hide her rage and fury, her hurt and pain. Her heart ached for a big black hole to crawl in so no one would see her tears or her fears. "Who is this woman and what is she doing in my hospital room? Is she here not only to take my Love but also to take my Hope as well? No one would be or could be that cruel. Could they?" These were all the random thoughts and questions that ran through her head. She was in dismay and did not really know how to respond. Faith felt like someone had just stabbed her in the heart. "How could Love be so cruel and selfish to bring another woman to the hospital, not only to see Hope, but to meet me? My baby is only a few hours old. These should be private moments shared between family—not some stranger you just met weeks prior. Who does that? Love! And her! She obviously has no morals or dignity. Common sense should tell her that now would not be a good time to visit. And she thinks she is going to be "step-mother" to my child—HA!" As random thoughts kept circling in her head, Faith knew exactly what needed to be done. Keep your friends close and your enemies closer. So she suppressed her feelings, put a smile on her face, had pleasantries and made the best of a very horribly uncomfortable situation.

Faith knew no one could give Hope the faith that he needed like she could. This was now her new life. She was new to the job of motherhood, but totally committed and up for the challenge to make it work with her new love, Hope—God's gift to her because of her strong will and determination. She refused to let anyone come and spoil her new found joy. She took pride in wrapping her baby in her arms. She pretended like everything and everyone else was non-existent.

Now here she stood, a mother, dejected and depressed at the reality of her situation. She maintained her faith that Hope would not suffer at the hands of misguided Love. Yet day by day as time passed, Love faded and Faith was left alone with Hope. The hope that everything will be alright—hope that the right decisions were made—hope that the road taken will someday lead to a light at the end of the tunnel, knowing the darkness felt at this moment in time was to remain for quite a while.

Faith anticipated that Love would take one look at Hope and be hooked, but it was Hope who took one look at Love and fell head over heels. What a hopeless situation: the voice of Love, the sight of a father figure, the smell of a lifetime commitment and the taste of happiness at his fingertips. It was clear at that moment, Hope would forever yearn for this person. He could not get enough; could not get enough of his **"father,"** his **"daddy,"** his *"Love."*

Faith and Love began to take on the challenge of parenthood. Faith began to realize more and more that she was going to be in for a long battle. Although they lived so close, she felt she had to beg Love to spend time with his son. All the stories of single parenthood that she read about and heard from others had now become her reality. What she saw her mother and other women in her family doing had now become her life. What would she do? She never imaged her life turning out like this. This was not a part of the "life" she envisioned.

Day by day, Faith and Hope grew closer and began to truly bond as mother and son. She embraced her new motherly role and took the good with the bad. Every day was a learning experience. Love embraced the title more than the role itself, which was not much different, from the nine months prior. So his actions did not come as much of a surprise. He was very proud to say he was a father but did not do much as a "dad" should.

Faith had no tolerance for that type of "fatherly" behavior. She was relentless. She called, she showed up, she argued and fought for what she wanted, which was for her child to grow up knowing, respecting and being around both his parents. After all, why shouldn't that be possible? It was not an unreasonable request. Even if they were not together, that should not stop Love from coming around, getting to know, and spending quality time with his son. It would be different if he was dead or in jail, but that was not the case. He lived right down the street. It was unacceptable to her that a person could be so close and yet so far toward their own flesh and blood. She did not give up or give in. She knew what she wanted and would exhaust every possibility before throwing in the towel. She was doing what she believed to be the right thing for Hope.

Nothing or no one can change someone who does not want to change. To try is a waste of time. Change must come from within a person and not from others. Many times we believe if we push hard enough, we will get another person to do as we want them to. That person may change for a while but in the end, that person will revert to being who he/she is until he/she is ready to acknowledge that he/she wants to change and why. We are merely here to support that person along the way.

Because Faith was so persistent and adamant, she, Love, and Hope began spending more time together. They began to look and feel like a family although they were not. They were still raising Hope as co-parents. However, the more time they spent together, the more the old flames started to rekindle. Uh oh, here we go again! The confusion between love and lust reared its ugly head, but the attraction could not be denied or ignored.

Romance and laughter were back! But this time there was an added member—Hope. He made them look at life differently, a bit more mature. It was time to put the immature behaviors aside and do what was and felt right. They decided to be a real family. By that time, Hope was two; Faith had found a job and moved into her own apartment. Love was not far behind. Through breakfast, lunch, and dinner, the trio moved together as a family. For a while, Faith was on top of the world. This was like a dream come true. Everything was falling into place as she had imagined. This was in fact the life she envisioned for herself and most importantly, for her son. Unfortunately, as time went on, reality became clearer. Deep down inside, the missing piece of the family puzzle was still there. Commitment still did not exist and Faith was still yearning for that more and more, with each passing day. Love had no intention on sealing this deal of family with matrimony and Faith had no desire to continue living the lie. The reality of true colors began to take a toll on the couple and their family life. They each seemed to be wanting more and expecting something that was not being provided. Little by little, distance became the way of dealing with the inconsistencies in their growing personalities and priorities.

"Having my children has changed my life in so many ways. I am more caring, more responsible, more conscientious, and overall, I am more appreciative of life. I work and live for them; they are a huge part of my life.

Kids require lots of time. My wife and I have much less personal time; but in the end, it is a sacrifice worth making!"

—Andre Dyer

Destiny Awaits

Why do people run when the going gets tough?
Running scared of their own shadow
Like groundhogs looking for the first sign of spring

Why do people run when the best is yet to come?
But the unknown is more terrifying
Than the bite after a bumble bee sting

Why do people run at the thought of failure?
At the thought of success?
Or at the thought of being blessed?

We run in fear, afraid of our tears
The lessons learned that got us burned
In preparation for what is to be
That thing called Destiny

So fear not for what He has in store
Is powerful enough to open all doors
Gateways and highways leading you to
A grand design made just for you

And, it may not be what you had in mind
But it came for a reason, so just take time
To explore unconditional love at the gate
Because low and behold, your destiny awaits!

—*Terryl Ebony*

CHAPTER 3:
Caught in the Middle

Constant arguments led to verbal and sometimes physical abuse, with no one willing to compromise but everyone wanting to be heard. Faith had no patience or tolerance for the unjust behaviors of Love; and therefore, she was usually the initiator of many of the altercations. She could not understand how someone could stand so near yet be so far from the one person who needed him most—Hope. It was years before she realized that the man she fell in love with was the splitting image of her own father's characteristics. He, too, was raised by both mother and father but for some unknown reason was not a family man himself. Both of these men brought children into the world, but did not want the responsibility behind it. They still wanted live the single life.

- -

The male and female species are very interesting. When seeking a mate, a male will normally gravitate to someone who reminds them of their mother. Females will turn to men who have characteristics like their father. These traits can be positive or negative. Interestingly enough, more often than not, as humans we tend to lean towards the negative. It probably would not start off that way in the beginning because the relationship is new. However, when the fresh layers begin to peel and the core of the person is revealed, if you are honest you will see many resemblances from your past.

- -

Well just as things did not work out with her mother and father, Faith knew her relationship with Love was not going to work out either. They both knew it but were too stubborn or too selfish to put an end to the long drawn out saga. So, it continued with Hope at the helm. Hope adored both his parents and had the dubious honor of hearing their yells, seeing their cries, feeling the tension, and sharing in their lies. He was caught in the middle.

- -

No relationship is perfect. There will be times when you will not agree. That disagreement should be kept between the two adults. Your child should not have to witness the arguments. Children are always the ones who suffer most when parents argue, whether they are arguing about the child or about something else. When you argue or fight in front of your child—regardless of whose fault or how the argument started—both of you have failed. Both of you now share equal responsibility in why your child has experienced this indiscretion.

When a child continues to witness such negative actions and behaviors especially when it is from their parents, it is not uncommon for them to begin to take personal responsibility for why these actions are occurring. They begin to rationalize to themselves how they have in some way contributed to or caused your feelings or behaviors, leaving them with a feeling of guilt, anger and confusion amongst others. Be careful and be observant. At this point, you may begin to notice a change in your child's behavior. It can also creep up on you without your even realizing it. The change in behavior may not all appear negative. Everyone masks his or her emotions differently. You may have two children experiencing the same hurt and confusion. One may play their emotions out by getting in trouble in school and the other may suppress their emotions by doing extremely well in school. Either one will prove to be destructive, in its own right and in its own time, if not discovered and effectively treated.

Remember, you are your child's first role model and teacher. As your child gets older and begins to build a family of his/her own, that child will emulate your behavior. So, here is a thought from your child, "You are my parents, and so if it is normal behavior for you, why would not it be normal behavior for me?"

- -

Watching the effects on the hopeful one gave Faith a renewed perspective. Her life was no longer her own. Her feelings were now secondary. Hope had to be her primary focus. She tried to convince Love of the same, but her rational thoughts were overshadowed by her screams and his inability to digest anything that did not start and finish with his name. So Hope remained in the middle of the ongoing saga and even at his tender age, he could feel the pull and the distance building between his parents. He, himself, began to become distant toward his parents. This is when Faith knew she had to put an end to this emotional rollercoaster. And still, her mind told her "Yes" but her heartstrings were saying "No".

The two continued in their dysfunctional relationship. They enjoyed their ups and wished away their downs. And just when Faith thought things could not get any worse, they did. She was pregnant . . .!

Faith discovered that she was expecting another hopeful bundle of joy. Although unexpected, she thought for sure this time things would be different. Love had matured some and he would not put her through the same turmoil as he did the last time. Although it was unplanned, she was somewhat excited and leery all at the same time. She began to rationalize in her head how everything would work itself out. Hope had recently turned four. Both parents were working. They were living on their own. What else was needed? In her mind. . . . Nothing! So cautiously, she broke the news to a doubtful Love. Once again, he was not sure how he felt about taking on yet another huge responsibility for the second time around. That would mean more of himself that he would have to sacrifice. After all, he still was not sure how he felt about the first one. He was still struggling with all that came along with being a father to Hope and a family man. Was he ready to do it all over again?

Faith, on the other hand, felt she was in a decent place. She was not completely happy, but she was not miserable either. She was content and taking life day by day. As the news of conception became reality, she was clear on what she wanted and what she did not. She knew that she would not survive nine months of the same agony that she went through before. And, she definitely did not want to bring another blessing into such chaos and dysfunction. Although she was against the idea of termination, she felt like her back was up against a wall. It would not be fair to anyone involved. She already experienced, first hand, what it was like going through nine months of pregnancy on her own. She would not be put in that situation again. She did not want the fate of Hope or the unborn child to be one that was filled with resentment. She knew they would suffer and that was not an acceptable outcome.

Again, very honest about his feelings, Love told her without doubt that there would be no promise or consideration of change. Faith knew she had a huge decision to make. It was like déjà vu. The conversation played over and over in her head, tearing her heart in two over the possibilities of making the wrong choice. Thoughts of a little Faith running around shadowing her mother's every move overwhelmed her mind and filled her up with joy. However, she then thought about Hope and what he went through before and after he came into the world. She would not wish that on anyone, especially a child. It was hard enough to look one child in the eye and see his hurt and pain, much less two. She could not do it. She would not do it. She also thought about what she went through and what she was still going through—the anger, the depression, the loneliness, the emptiness, and the pain. Every angle that she looked at, the pros never outweighed the cons. So as far as she was concerned, there was nothing left to do. She made the decision to terminate her pregnancy. Although it hurt, she felt she made the right decision and even though she had to live with the question of "what if" for the rest of her life, she would rather deal with that than the depression and disrespect that followed Hope's conception.

At that point, Faith new this was the end for her and Love. She knew she would never look at him the same again. That loss would forever be a barrier between them. She also knew she did not want to wait a lifetime for him to decide that she and Hope were enough for him. So, they separated although there were still strong feelings shared. They even found themselves reliving some intimate moments every now and again.

Through the break-up, they tried to maintain a civil understanding, but that, too, was more difficult for Faith than for Love. However, she knew it was for the best. She knew she could not continue a life with someone who was that self-centered, and she gave him respect because he was finally honest about how he felt and what he wanted—and did not want. However, deep down inside she knew she wanted more for her and her son. She wanted a family that consisted of mother, father, and child. And although she let him go with words, in her heart she still held on to love. What she could not hold on to was the way he began to treat and distance himself from his son. After all, he was the innocent one. She could not understand why she had to continually be on top of him to see or inquire about his child. "Do you not love him? Do you not want to be a part of his life? Are you making him suffer for what you and I are going through?" These were all thoughts running through her mind, day in and day out. Faith had to beg and argue for money to help raise Hope. She never thought in a million years that she would be going through this. She never thought that the man she loved and had a child for would treat them so badly. But, this was now her reality.

Faith began working extra hard to build and sustain her relationship with Hope. She could feel him slipping away. He did not want to talk and on occasions he would display his anger by throwing temper tantrums, banging his head against the wall, or punching something with his fists. By the time Hope was four, Faith knew she had a lot of explaining to do, but more importantly she wanted him to know he could count on her for an honest answer. She wanted to reassure him that he was wanted, loved and the center of her world through all the chaos. Love took a different route. He pulled further away from the hopeful bliss that should have brought the two closer together. This only made situations worse.

Ladies, usually men are very honest and consistent in what they do and say. We tend to ignore them though—their words, their signs, and their actions—which usually leaves us feeling betrayed and hurt, but we should not because we were warned. Do not ignore what has been defined for you, and then blame them for not telling you. Directly or indirectly, the message was sent. Now, what you do with the information is what makes the difference in what happens next in your life. Just know that whatever happens, you have to own it. That choice and responsibility is on you not him.

- -

With each passing day, it became more and more clear that there was no Hope on Love's priority list. This was not easy. Layers and layers of selfish thoughts and deception—just like an onion being peeled away to revealing all the lies, dishonesty, treachery, infidelity, and pain mixed with faithful sorrow. Love's captivating ways made many overlook his obvious selfish behavior. Faith tried everything she could think of to get Love to pay attention to Hope. She asked; she begged; she yelled; she screamed; she cursed and carried on, hoping that something she would do would get him to act differently towards his son. Nothing worked! And when he did choose to come around, it would not last for long. Love became known to Faith as the "revolving door dad"—one day he was there and the next day he was not. He popped in and out of Hope's life sometimes for weeks or months at a time.

Although Faith wanted a family, she began to come to terms with the fact that it would not be with Love. He, too, had to now face the reality that Faith would no longer endure the hurt and pain that came with his unfaithful and selfish love. Only the Lord knew how they survived as long as they did. This relationship was definitely irrational. Faith always wondered why people subjected themselves to such pain and anguish, and here she was experiencing it firsthand. She came to the conclusion that love had no rhyme or reason. It was at that moment, when Love realized that Faith and Hope were the family he really wanted to be with, but it was too late. Faith had begun slipping away. Her love for him had started to fade. Her heart was filled with hurt, disgust and at times hatred because of what he had put her through and how he was treating Hope. Some things were just unacceptable.

Love found out that someone else began filling the void where love, happiness and concern use to live. Faith had a new friend who became her listening partner and distraction away from the chaos. The two became closer and began spending more time together. It was not long before the unintentional attraction started to surface. They tried to fight it for quite some time but after a while, the feeling of new comfort vs. old arguments won. Who would have thought she would fall in love again? This would have been great except for the fact that her new confidant was also Love's friend. This was a complication she never expected, nor did she want. It was a difficult situation all around. Deep down Love was still very present in her heart. He was the first man she gave and shared her ALL with, the man who gave her Hope, and the man who brought out her best and her worst. However, the feeling, attention, and attraction she felt with her new friend could not be ignored either.

Love did not give up easily and the obvious questions of "What if" began to plague Faith's mind. The echoes of comments, advice and sneering only complicated matters. What if things could work out with her Love? Maybe he really has changed? What if Mommy, Daddy and child really could survive under one roof? Then she began to think of the more realistic "what ifs". What if we argued for the rest of our lives? What if he is never ready to commit? What if we killed each other? Where would her Hope be? What would happen to him?

It got to a point where Faith was very confused. She put herself in a position where she felt she was in love with two people at the same time. How could this be? How did she get here? This was unfamiliar territory for her and she knew she had to do something. She could not eat or sleep. She began losing weight because she did not know how to handle the situation. Should she interrupt what could be the "traditional" family life? Should she risk the criticism of friends and family, or jeopardize her new found happiness for the sake of all others? So many questions weighed heavily on her heart and her mind, so she decided to follow her gut. She had tried for many years to move forward with Love; she knew deep down it was time to let go and give something new a chance. She knew the love triangle was not her, but after everything Love had done to her, she started to become him—a liar, a cheater, selfish and thoughtless. Faith looked in the mirror and took some time to reflect. She knew what she had to and wanted to do. Faith made the decision to close a memorable chapter in her life called Love. They had years of faithful bliss, combined with the ups and downs of love and happiness, mixed with pain and sorrow. The two had come to a crossroads. What started out as faithful love filled with devotion and respect turned out to be a chapter of deception and heartbreak. Where once they had nothing in common, Hope—would now be that link bonding the two forever.

Meanwhile, Faith had her new friend to keep her mind occupied. For a while, there were still lots of confusion in her head as to whether she made the right decision. Returning to the familiar place of comfort would be easy, but it would not bring happiness.

- -

You have a decision and you do not know what to do. Do not follow your heart—It is too emotional. Do not follow your mind—It is too logical. Follow your gut—It is the only thing that is not biased and unconditional. And, sometimes the hardest thing you ever have to do can turn out to be the best thing for you in the long run. Change is often a big adjustment and many people are afraid or intimidated by it. But once you get the hang of it, it is like tying your shoes or riding a bike—easy. A large part of success is having the faith and courage to step out of your comfort zone and try something different.

- -

The whispers and rumors from friends, family and spectators were severe, but she was determined to get past it all. None of that mattered to her. The resilience in Faith was remarkable. She had dealt with criticism and judgment from the day she was born. So why would this chapter in her life be any different? It was actually to be expected. However, as each day went by and she thought about the circumstances of her past, present and future, she opted for her future—not only for her but for Hope. She was ready and armored with a new love, hope, family and friends who would not let her fall or succumb to the nuances of immature gossip. This protective shield gave her strength and empowerment to endure everything that would happen next. This man gave new meaning to the glow in her eye and the light that shined on Hope. It all felt right.

To those parents that are no longer together:
Put whatever feelings you have about each other aside and
keep your child's life as stable as possible.

No matter what, respect each other and be civil at all times
in the presence of your child. The house rules should not
change because you are no longer together.

Be careful what you say about each other in front of your
child; choose your words wisely.

—Pamela Brewington-Lawson

Emptiness

I wake up every morning and look around
Noticing every picture and every sound
I am conscious and alert to what is going on
But the emptiness I feel is like a death to mourn

To my friends, I am happy and jolly as can be
Hanging out and partying for all to see
But deep down inside I am traveling a dark road
I feel like a time bomb about to explode

Wrestling with the image of who they think I am
Versus the person inside that is still a boy, not quite a man
Yet the responsibilities are piling and the job is getting tough
But no one seems to notice or call my bluff

So I continue to smile, joke, and play
When in reality, I am hurting and crying but do not want to
say
Afraid of losing the image and people finding out
That the person before them has no real clout

But how long can I hide from this feeling inside
I am losing my way because of my pride
I do not ask for help. People think I am in control
But this emptiness I feel touches my soul

From sun up to sun down, it is all a façade
I am lost and I am angry and I do not know why
My life seems glamorous from the outside—in
But from where I sit, there is no love within

The emptiness is growing because I have not changed my ways
Living a double life on alternate days
I have to stay true to who I am and what I believe
If my ultimate goal is to succeed

I cannot continue to live with this emptiness
Life is too short to lack real happiness
It is not about doing for he or for she
In the end, it is just about me.

By Terryl Ebony

CHAPTER 4:
Changing Faces

Love, like people, has many faces. Every day being a toss-up between Dr. Jekyll and Mr. Hyde, and if you are lucky you were blessed by both people on the same day. The life of Dr. Jekyll is positive, kind, and compassionate. Mr. Hyde is cold, inconsiderate, and selfish.

- -

What is it about this combination that most find attractive? Do the qualities of Dr. Jekyll outshine those of Mr. Hyde, therefore overlooking the obvious negative traits? I wonder. We hear the saying way too often that good girls like bad boys. We must begin to examine why. With the knowledge that every individual is different, I am led to believe that there is something either lacking in the partners that women are attracted to or something present in their upbringing that they are used to, that define the men that women choose. So it could be that you did not grow up with a male figure around, so you are now searching for what you believe you are missing. Or you have seen this behavior in your past and have been conditioned to believe it is normal and therefore acceptable behavior. Either way it is not good for you. In a relationship, both the male and female should be treated with respect and are there to uplift each other.

- -

On a good day, Love will shine like the sun in the sky on the hottest summer day. You would be sheltered and covered with warmth, affection, sensitivity, and humor. You would be overshadowed by the here and now with no thought of tomorrow; free to smile and laugh and experience his most intimate side. This is the Dr. Jekyll behavior—Love at his best. He is infectious—keeps you wanting more and more. There is an enticing behavior about him. You do not even see it coming, it just creeps up on you and before you know it, you are sucked in . . . . hooked!

Love is also very charming and adventurous. Most people find him attractive, engaging and fun to be around. He is the type of person who will fly by the seat of his pants, living on the edge of the world for today as if tomorrow does not exist. That is fine with him. At sixteen years old, some would even say and that is the way it should be.

This is who Faith fell in love with at age fifteen. These were all the qualities she was looking for in a man. It was odd because they really had nothing in common except the fact that they lived on the same block and shared mutual friends. They did not even like each other in the beginning, but then they became friends and the feelings started to grow. It took a while, but Love had won her over. He had her mind, body and soul. There was very little she could do to get from under his grasp. His charm and sensitivity would win her over every time.

Love is a good looking man with captivating eyes and dimpled cheeks—all the things that set the tone for love, lust, and lies. He lures you in with no thought of how his actions will affect you or anyone else. At first sight, his qualities are appealing and quite charismatic. When you look further and get to know him, you begin to realize that all is not as it seems. You slowly begin to see the signs of Mr. Hyde.

Mr. Hyde will sneak up on you. You will not be prepared or impressed. It is a complete 180 degree turn from Dr. Jekyll. Love is now filled with deceit. Lies are told to protect his secrets and falsify his good deeds. The look in his eyes is now filled with selfishness and ego. It is all about the benefit and betterment of Love. Nothing or no one else matters as long as his needs are met. So, the questions begin: Who is he trying to impress? His friends? His family? Or maybe himself? Whatever the impression, it was not a pretty one.

While living in the moment, Love wanted to help others. If you needed a favor, you knew for the most part he was dependable. This satisfied his need to be liked and adored by others, giving him a superficial form of self-gratification. However, there was an exception. The rule mainly applied to friends. Family, in his eyes, was an afterthought. This laid the groundwork for his priorities. Professionally, Love is a hard worker. He takes his job very seriously. That was definitely one of his priorities. His love for sports remained a priority. No matter how beat up he got, no matter how sore his body was, Love made sure that he was on the football field every Sunday and any other night that required practice time. His passion for fashion was clearly priority. All the latest styles and fashion designers made their way into his closet. Fun in the sun is a definite priority, not to be forgotten. This is what he lives for. All these things are a priority. So where did family fit in? Or did it fit in at all? People said he just needed time to grow up and mature. That is a plausible possibility but he could not explain that to a baby, a toddler, an adolescent, or a teenager. These priorities held him back from the biggest priority of all—Hope.

They say men mature later than women, so we tend to pass many of the male actions off as immaturity. But at what age or stage in life does immaturity run its course? Does it ever? Or does immaturity now become an excuse for selfish behavior? What happens to all the lives that are affected by this behavior—family, children, friends, love interests? People should just avoid these aspects of life if they are not ready to commit to them, whether male or female. There is too much at stake. You must realize that this behavior will only end in self-destruction.

As Love battled to find the one he wanted to spend the rest of his life with, he spent a lot of time dating and getting to know various women. There were times when Hope was privy to these women. It was a very unhealthy way of life for a child. It also meant that Hope had yet someone else that he had to fight for his daddy's love, affection, and time. On the surface he was grateful for whatever time he could get with his father. Then, Love began spending time with a friend from the past that already had children of her own. The more time they spent together, the more Hope would shut down. Unfortunately, Love could not see the resentment in Hope's eyes. Hope would not verbalize his feelings but they came out in his actions. Hope went as far as to tell the Dean of his school that his name was Love when he got in trouble. This was a clear cry for daddy's attention yet, Love thought it was admiration of a son wanting to be like his father. He repeatedly made excuses for Hope's negative behavior and his own parental neglect.

Excuses and deflection are clear signs of guilt and irresponsibility. It is hard for most people to admit they are wrong. It is even harder to admit that you are not handling your responsibilities as a parent. Parents are very territorial and we want to believe that we are doing what is best for our children. However, this is not always the case. Many times we must take a step back and look at the situation at hand with a clear vision and open mind. It is only then that we will be able to see our flaws, accept constructive feedback from others, and understand the true needs of our children.

"Let the world know you as you are, not as you think you should be because sooner or later, if you are posing, you will forget the pose, and then where are you?"

—*Fanny Brice*

Little Do They Know

All alone is how I feel
In a house with no appeal
Everyone here thinks they know me well
But little do they know, there is not much to tell

This is because they do not know me
They just know who they see
They are trying to take over the life I am trying to lead
But little do they know, they will not succeed

'Cause I am me as you can see
And me being who I am
Considers myself special indeed

And no one can change that, no matter how they try
Try to change me into someone I am not
I am not a little girl so why do not they stop
Stop treating me like the baby I was years ago
But treat me like the young adult I'll be tomorrow
Adults! What little they really know . . . .

—*Terryl Ebony*

CHAPTER 5:
I am who I am

Whether through her fashion, her hairstyles, her facial expressions, hand gestures or her vocals, Faith always made a statement. How she feels is clear from first approach, often written invisibly across her face—nothing hidden in her words but often misconstrued by her appearance. From the earliest of life, people would misinterpret who she was and what she was all about. Everyone had their own theory as to where she would end up and what she would become. They applied their opinion to all aspects of her life: social, professional, personal, and parental. Her future was pre-cast in stone by others. They thought they knew everything there was to know about this brown-skinned, short haired, seductive girl with the "tell all" mouth. Because she was outgoing and wanted to hang out with friends, she was predestined to be a follower down the wrong path as opposed to leading the way for others. Because she gave birth early in life, her career goals were now limited opposed to limitless. Because she was independent, she was not entitled to be loved by a strong man. Because all of the above coupled with the fact that she was aggressively opinionated, her parental skills were predetermined inadequate.

- -

Very simply put, do not judge a book by its cover. You may be giving up on a prize possession because you cannot see past the outer layer. It is what is inside that counts most. Dig deeper; get to know people for who they really are inside, and you may be pleasantly surprised. The one you judge could very well be the one that has the wisdom, the confidence, the professionalism or the friendship you may need one day. You never know who is who.

- -

Well, their assumptions could not have been further from the truth. With every passing year, Faith went on to prove them wrong despite the odds. And although she could hear their whispers and feel their negative thoughts, she would never be deterred. She knew her heart, she knew her mind, and she definitely knew her ambitions held endless possibilities and unforeseen realities. She also knew the inner beauty she held would one day shine through and everyone would see her as she saw herself. She had faith. She was Faith!

Faith is realistically direct. She is the kind of person who would give you the best advice—THE TRUTH—whether you wanted to hear it or not. Most people do not like the truth or they want it to be sugar coated to fit their picture perfect reality, which is often warped. Faith had no time for these illusions and no problem verbalizing her beliefs. This often made her unpopular and got her into plenty of trouble, but she did not care. She stood strong beside her beliefs, beside her comments and her actions. Whatever resulted, she was prepared to handle.

- -

Facing reality is often a hard process. Sometimes it even hurts. But the longer it takes you to listen and accept it, the longer it will take you to Live it, Learn it, and Deal with it! The Truth can be a harsh reality! Embrace it; do not run from it. Be happy if you are surrounded by people who will tell you the truth and be honest with you regardless of how it may make you feel. Just remember that most of the time, there is a tactful way that the truth can be told. But in the event that you must be blunt, go for it because the truth is better than a lie any day.

- -

Faith had a passion for being the best at whatever she took on to conquer. She was always engaged in a new project that challenged and stimulated her mind. She was not afraid to try anything. She was not afraid of the success or the failure that may have followed, and she encouraged everyone she knew to do the same. She thrived under pressure. She did not become unraveled or unnerved at the unknown or the deadline.

Faith was the opposite of Love in that she did not engage in many friendships as she saw them as a hindrance. She always had a select few friends in whom she confided. This was her Innerbeauty Sister Circle. These few had everything she needed. They all possessed different qualities she needed to keep her grounded when she felt either encouraged or discouraged in anyway. Outside of that, there was not much time for all the other confusion that came along with being a socialite. There was too much to accomplish with little time to succeed. This brought out her determination and passion. She knew what she wanted and went after it. Some would call it aggressive. She called it life.

Although family meant a lot to Faith so did her career. She loved to work. It took her awhile to figure out what her purpose was in life. After the birth of her son and the destruction of her relationship, it became clear to her that her mission was to help others, especially children and parents going through similar ordeals. So, she dedicated a lot of time to supporting efforts and creating opportunities to help parents, teachers, and other educators understand, develop, and stimulate the minds of our youth. Thankfully, she had a different perspective on the makeup of mankind and was able to view people from the inside out and not the other way around. Faith also spent a lot of time helping parents who struggled with their children to help them find a better way to communicate, see things from the child's point of view. Just as important, she helped parents see how their past may be affecting their ability to make the best decisions not only for their child but also for themselves. Faith was convinced that just like any relationship people must know and love themselves before they can begin to understand and effectively help their children. Faith provided that safe haven for both parents and children. Her ears were the place they could reveal all their inhibitions, fears, desires and goals. Her mouth spoke the truth but more importantly the questions she posed made them often find the truth for themselves.

In the beginning, parents found it difficult to pay for such a service, especially people in the minority communities. Most of them had never heard of a Family Life Coach. They were not cognizant of how all of their outside distractions interfered and affected not only the parent/child relationship but the two individuals as well. However, each time they left Faith, they felt like they had achieved a better understanding of who they were and how they could be more effective as parents. They began to see for themselves the positive differences in their child(ren) and within themselves, whether it was pertaining to school, home, careers, or relationships. Faith was there to help people re-design their lives. After a while, the word spread and before you knew it, the people who did not think they could afford her services found a way. They saw the significant value in what she offered.

At times her career interfered with her domestic responsibilities as traditionally designed to be the expected role of the woman. Spending time with family was second nature. Cooking and cleaning was often that of another language—a trait she wished rubbed off from her parents'. She did what was needed to get by, but a maid every now and then would not have been so bad, if money permitted. This was her biggest challenge in her relationship, and she eventually learned that she had to put as much effort in that as she did with everything else in order to create a balance.

Women are becoming more and more independent. This should not overshadow the need for love and companionship. This should not be an excuse why being with a man is no longer important, spending quality time with your children becomes secondary, taking care of your home gets put on the back burner or socializing becomes an afterthought. These are all very crucial aspects of a woman's life. No one is more important than the other. They are all there to keep you balanced.

Faith is a realist and believes there is a time and a place as well as a reason and a season for everything. There once was a time for fun and spontaneity. That was a large part of who she was prior to giving birth. After which, her life drastically changed. Faith was still fun, but now she had new priorities and a new reason for living. That reason gives her Hope.

Faith is to believe what you do not see;
the reward of this faith is to see what you believe.
—Saint Augustine—

From: Me   *To: You*

Dedicated to my son

Lift your head high and walk proud
Do not mumble, talk loud
Try your best in all you do
Motherly advice from me: to you

You meet acquaintances your whole life
But for that special someone you call your wife
Respect her, love her, and always be true
Womanly advice from me: to you

False pride tears people apart
Be true to yourself and follow your heart
Do not be afraid to admit the wrong you do
Friendly advice from me: to you

Know that sincerity will open the door
Honesty and respect will bring you more
Money to invest and spend—that is true
Professional advice from me: to you

Many people seek eternal happiness
Seek God first to fulfill that emptiness
For tomorrow is not promised to but a few
Spiritual advice from me: to you

Grow, learn, and experience what you can
Be a father, a daddy, and a family man
Courage and strength will see you through
Fatherly advice from me: to you

—Terryl Ebony

CHAPTER 6:
Her Prodigy

Hope was an innocent being already seeking Faith and Love from day one. Faith often stared in disbelief at Hope, a mirror image of the man that fathered him. Amazed at how life was created—the life that "she" had created—her prodigy. She was in awe that this 7lb, 19 ¾ inch baby came from her body. Never in her wildest dreams did she imagine this was even possible. Growing up she did not think children were going to be a part of her life and look at her now—such a proud mother.

Day by day as she watched him grow, his hugs were infectious. They kept her wanting more. Spending every available moment talking, laughing, singing, and dancing hopeful tunes that bonded the two from birth were only a stepping stone for what lied ahead. Having Faith kept Hope grounded but was not enough to keep him from seeking Love. He craved an attention in Love that no one could replace. Unfortunately, Love was too blind to notice how much Hope needed what should have come so naturally: presence, attention, and communication, all the things as important, if not more important than actual love itself. So why cannot Love look into Hope's eyes and see his desires?

- -

Children speak through their eyes and their cries. They speak through their motions and devotions. They speak through their words and their tones. If you listen carefully and pay attention, it will not be that difficult to figure out what they are trying to say. But that is the problem. Many parents do not listen; they often assume, usually jumping to the wrong conclusion. Many parents are often defensive and take offense to constructive feedback. This defense mechanism is the norm but it is far from normal. Yes, we like to think we are doing what is best for our children; however, this same defense mechanism is also counter-productive. It clouds your judgment and prohibits you from making better, smarter, and more productive decisions for or about your child. The best thing you can do for your child is to be open minded. You may be surprised at how your outcomes change (for the better) when you open up to unknown possibilities and unfamiliar dynamics. Sometimes you have to put yourself in your child's shoes and get out of your own. The perception of new eyes often clarifies what has been blinding you all the while. Most importantly, listen and observe your child. They are looking to you for understanding not assumptions.

- -

As he got older and his bones began to stretch, so did his personality. He showed signs of sensitivity, love, and compassion. Humor and entertainment came natural. He loved to dance and make people laugh. His smile and loving bear hug would melt your heart. He loved cartoons and animation. The combination of these artistic expressions manifested itself in his personality.

However, the Dr. Jekyll and Mr. Hyde personality apparently ran in the family because he was also a people pleaser, but when he got upset—look out! It was hard to stop him or settle him down. Even in his toddler years, Faith knew he was going to be a handful and it was not going to be an easy task. He was so smart but he had a temper. When time came to attend school, his behavior presented many problems.

As Hope began to speak and learn, it was clear that he would be very loud and outspoken. He was very technical and literal. You could not paraphrase with him. Say what you mean and mean what you say was his mentality. He thrived on facts and had no problem debating those facts. His articulate speech made him stand out in school. His grades were outstanding when his mind was right, but began to yo-yo when the reality of life began to take control over his emotions.

He loved to read and write—writing short stories about fictional war heroes and the battles they had to conquer. Faith often wondered if he felt those stories mirrored his life and the battles he faced. Although she was proud and encouraged his works of art, she was torn and tried to understand the underlying messages hidden within his words.

Everyone perceived the academic side of him to be who he was and what he would become. Some already deemed him "The Future President of the United States" all because of his demeanor and the way he spoke out on that which he was passionate. But there was more to speak about, yet he would never go there. He knew what he was feeling, knew the words to say, but it just would not happen. All the Love he did not receive—all the attention, all the calls, all the gifts, all the hugs, and all the firsts that he was not privy to broke his heart and broke him down. There was a part of him missing, a part he *thought* could not be found until he found Love. Eventually he had to learn not to search for Love but to find Hope.

As usual, Faith remained optimistic that Love would change at least for the sake of Hope. And although he rarely came around, it made her day to see those hopeful eyes shine bright like the sun in the sky and the smile that spread from ear to ear when Love was present. You knew it meant everything to Hope—whether for a minute, an hour, or a day, he enjoyed every moment with his Love.

- -

Parents do not realize the lasting effects they have on their children. That time you spend with them is priceless. You cannot redo it and it will not come again. So, take advantage of it, learn from it, and enjoy it. Your children are hanging on to your every limb, looking at your every smile or frown, and digesting your every word. So be careful. Make sure the hand you raise is done in love; make sure you smile more than you frown; and last but not least, make sure you watch what you say and the way you say it. This applies especially when the two parents are no longer involved. It is very easy to make the other parent look or sound inferior without even trying and it may not be your goal, but that can be how your child perceives it.

You must think before you speak, especially when you are upset. You do not want to send the wrong message to your child. "I said it because I was angry" is not a good or valid excuse for hurting your child. What needs to be understood is that saying negative things against the other parent hurts both you and your child in the long run. You may ask, how does it hurt me? Well, if you care about your child and your child is hurting, then in turn you will begin to feel that pain along with the pain of knowing that it was your words or actions that caused your child's pain in the first place. Yes, the other parent may have sparked "your" initial hurt and frustration, but it was "your" words that sparked your child's initial hurt and frustration. In the end, the hurt that you caused will be what your child will remember, and your child will eventually turn on you. Think about it.

- -

Many people view success by the amount of money or assets they possess. My biggest asset is my son. He has given my life the most value and my heart the greatest treasure imaginable.

Cherish every moment with your children. Do not take your time with them for granted. They grow up so quickly that by the time you catch your breath from that day in the park, they will be teenagers and then off to college and a life all their own.

Love them! Listen to them! Learn from them!

—Terryl Ebony

Through the Eyes of Heart Break

I am helpless as I watch beyond the eyes of the little him and
the little me
I am hopeless as I fear the truth as he would see
Random thoughts of lawyers and doctors, is who he could be
My heart breaks as I look and see

I have visions of love and laughter, from my dear
Compassion is rich as I hold him near
Not even Mother's love can stop his tears
My heart breaks as I watch in fear

I can dream of life where he should feel no pain
Only wishful thoughts gone down the drain
Hurt and sorrow like clouds and rain
My heart breaks as reality remains

I sense that He is trapped like an animal in a cage
Fighting emotions of anger and rage
Why should he suffer at his tender age?
My heart breaks and I AM OUTRAGED!

—Terryl Ebony

CHAPTER 7:
Prostituting for Love

A pimp—selfishly thinking about himself, his needs, his wants—not considering those who work so hard to serve and please him. A prostitute—insecure, lacking confidence and self-esteem; needs to feel wanted and looking for love. This is relationship between Love and Hope.

- -

Many things are passed down from generation to generation: looks, wealth, etc. Some people only focus on the obvious, the things they can identify with or see with their own eyes. But, there is so much more. There is such a power in words and emotions that many tend to ignore or deny. And there is a power in the physical being that many do not even see. Your children see; they learn; they adapt (sometimes in good ways and sometimes in bad); they are strong; but they can be vulnerable. Children are always seeking your guidance and acceptance, and when you are not there for them, they find it in someone else or something else. And, many instances that someone or something else is not necessarily positive. Your children view your abandonment as a personal attack on them. This lowers their self-esteem and heightens their distrust toward mankind.

- -

Although he is well into his teens, Hope's prostitution started when he was a toddler. His constant struggle of a hopeful Love reached an all-time high. Hope had to become resourceful and skillful to achieve his goal for Love's attention. A claim of war had been staked. Hope would stop at nothing to get the love that was so deserved and rightfully his for the taking.

Some prostitute for money or drugs; others prostitute for love—and Hope was no different. Love was the apple of his eye, and he would do whatever it took to get a piece of that forbidden fruit. So day in and day out he bared himself; he bared his soul for the attention he wanted, hoping one day Love would take notice. But like a pimp on the street, Love could not see beyond his own wants and desires which left a vulnerable, sad, hurt, Hope—full of growing resentment in one hand—longing to be needed in the other. Love would always throw him little crumbs; spend a little time; call every now and again; and even purchase an occasional gift. In the beginning, Hope would scramble for the crumbs and hold on to those moments for dear life. But as he grew he wanted and required more.

Still eager to succeed the everlasting battle of Love, Hope enticed Love with evenings of seduction. He filled his plate with honesty and trust with the hope that Love would bare his soul leaving him with words of consistency and stability. Week after week Hope would try to romance Love with tender gestures, hoping he would eventually take him under his wing, guide him and teach him to fly. Instead, Hope slowly came to the realization that he would never be enough to fill Love's appetite for fun, desire, or selfish love. There would always be someone or something more important, something to stand in the way, something to diminish Hope's pull on Love's heart strings.

Little by little, parents, teachers, family members, even friends slowly chip away at a child's self-esteem. When a child is ignored, that child begins to feel inadequate, blameful, and even shameful at times. It becomes more difficult for that child to know who he/she is. Inhibitions increase and self-confidence decreases. That child becomes aimless and an attention seeker. Eventually, that child is labeled "troubled youth".

A child's actions are the result of learned behavior, especially in the early years. This learned behavior can either increase or decrease one's self-esteem. Simultaneously, it can either have a negative or a positive impact on a child's life. Truth be told—the impact is usually one with negative results. I will begin to share with you a few examples of what can take place when a child lacks the attention, support, and guidance he/she needs and what lengths that child will go to—to get it.

Hoping that the ultimate sacrifice would bring endless love, the revelations began. Piece by piece, layer after layer, Hope was stripped of all innocence. Love was given all of what should be desired but blinded by a selfish eye he did not notice. He did not see Hope's nakedness, his vulnerability, his dependency or his obvious need for love and attention. Hopeful spirits of a bared soul for a Love that was only but a dream left a darkened place in the heart of one with low self-esteem.

Thinking back to when Hope was two years old, energetic and accustomed to his inner circle, he began to show anti-social behavior. Crying at the sight of man-kind became his way of expressing himself. Could this be because he was not accustomed to seeing men . . . . a man . . . . his father? Anything is possible. So, Faith enrolled him in school so that he could begin to socialize with other people and children his own age. Yet every morning for six months, he would cry and throw a tantrum upon entering the building. It took a while before Faith realized that it was not the people he was afraid of, but it was the fear of being left behind or forgotten, a feeling he knew all too well every time Love left his side not to return for days.

- -

Children learn safety and abandonment at a very early age. Do not take for granted that because your child can not speak that he/she does not understand. Not only does the child understand, but his/her feelings are just as sharp as any adult's. The difference is that you know how to express your feelings. The child's only learned outlet is through crying and you are wondering why.

- -

At age four, Faith's new love interest had taken on more and more of the fatherly role for Hope. At one point he wanted to call him "Pop". Of course, Love decided that was inappropriate and had forbidden Hope to do so again. Once again, Love wanted the name and the title without the responsibility. One would think, this would be a wake-up call to Love that he should start doing the things that a father is supposed to do, this way Hope would not think of someone else taking that spot. But, that did not happen.

There was another moment when Hope was still turning tricks, still seeking this parental comfort, still seeking Love's guidance and reassurance that he was wanted and desired. With the anticipation of stirring attention from the attracted one,

Hope proceeded to display his anger and growing frustration in school. When questioned by the Dean and the Principal about whom he was and why he was behaving so erratically, his response was, "My name is Love." Knowing that Hope had crossed their paths previously, the authority figures knew he was not being truthful and again could not understand his behavior. Anticipating that Faith could shed light on this puzzling situation, she was called in for a conference. Of course Faith, knowing what Hope was going through, understood immediately what had transpired. She explained the dilemma to all involved. They were able to relate and now understood why a 7-year-old child refused to recite his correct name. He was reprimanded and held accountable for his behavior. However, when Love found out about what had happened, he was in complete denial and made excuses for Hope's actions. He stated there is nothing wrong with a child wanting to emulate his father. He insisted this was normal behavior. Yes, under different circumstances this may be considered normal, but Faith knew, without a doubt, that this was a hopeful cry for help. It did not occur to Love that this display of falsification was an alternative means to an end. This was Hope's way of trying everything possible to get Love to spend more time with him and THEN maybe, just maybe if he liked what he saw, he would want to be more like him. Love's rationale was more believable to him because it would mean he did not have to accept responsibility for not being around.

- -

Parents: more often than not our children are talking to us in code, not because they want to because they do not know any better. You have to pay attention and learn the different ways your child communicates with you. Every child is different and their form of communication may differ as well. If you have more than one child in the house, do not think that their communication will be the same. If it is, great! But, more than likely, it will be different, so do not pre-judge and assume they will all communicate in the same way.

In this case, you have a child who claims he is his father and in other cases your child may cry, sing, get straight A's in school, over eat, under eat, or any other countless forms of expression and communication. So pay attention! If you miss it or misinterpret it, that could make the difference between saving your child from the hardship and having to clean up after the hardship.

- -

Getting desperate and feeling as if time was running out, Hope started to resort to other coping mechanisms that would possibly yield him the results he wanted. Hope began to play the defiant card. At 8, he made it clear Faith's new friend had become his role model. He no longer had respect for Love although he still loved him. He became that person who paid attention to him and gave him the things he deemed important at the time.

All of this had come to light and should have been another wakeup call for Love, but again he made excuses for Hope's remarks. He did not believe nor could he understand why Hope would say he had lost respect for his father. He thought he deserved his son's respect and admiration. Why? He definitely had not earned it. But because Hope still cared for Love and still yearned for that relationship, he would never express his true feelings to him directly. Hope feared that he would hurt Love's feelings and then their relationship would be even worse. Hope went as far to say that he believed Love would "suspend him" from his home if he hurt his feelings. He equated the situation as if he were being reprimanded in school. So, he preferred not to tell him how he really felt. In the back of his mind, he hoped that his acts of defiance would cause Love to open his eyes and pay attention. However, Love did not know how "to read" Hope's defiance, facial expressions or underlying remarks. This was a craft that took Faith years to perfect. Love could not learn this skill overnight. Instead, he told himself that the love he felt for his son was enough.

Faith was heartbroken over all the back and forth. She could not understand how a man could treat his flesh and blood this way, especially his first born. There were so many lingering questions but at the end of the day all that was left were two people, mother and child—hurt, confused and angry. Love's behavior toward Hope brought out her worse characteristics. She did not care what she said, what she did or how she behaved. All she knew was that she and her child were in pain because of him and he had to pay. He would not continue to pimp her son day in and day out, using him for his own selfish wants, then leaving him by the way side to fend for himself until the next time he had use for him. That was totally unacceptable; she had to put an end to the craziness. So Love was eventually banned from seeing Hope. Faith made the decision that it would be less painful for Hope not to see Love at all, than to see him every now and then and be left with the empty feeling of not knowing when he would see him again, and be filled with broken promises. She did not understand why her son had to endure such a life. Her thinking was out of sight, out of mind. After all, that is the way it was for her and her father.

As the years went by, Faith and Hope made the best of what they had. Although Faith had moved on and found another love, it did not fulfill Hope's needs for the same. He tried to welcome his new male role model with open arms and loved the time they spent together, but found it hard to accept from someone else what he felt his father should provide. Being an only child made matters worse. At times, Hope felt a great sense of loneliness and boredom. He began to find creative ways to entertain himself. The problem with that was those creative ways was usually destructive and sometimes dangerous.

Living with a working single parent, at age ten, Hope began to do things like drill holes in the walls because the drill was in sight. This could have been very dangerous if the drill had fallen or him or if he had drilled a body part. There was another incident when Hope lit a book on fire for no reason. He did not think anything of it until the flames became more than he could handle, so he threw the book out of his bedroom window. Hope thought the wind would extinguish the flames and squash the situation. Unfortunately, what he did not realize was that the burning book fell unto to some leaves by the basement door. The boiler room was on the other side. Thankfully, a neighbor was outside and saw the burning book being tossed out the window and notified Hope and the fire department immediately. Faith was terrified and furious at the same time. She began to lose confidence in her ability to raise Hope. She just knew the police were going to arrest her and cart Hope off to foster care. By the grace of God, everything worked out well, but that was just another example of how idle time could have gone very wrong for both Hope and Faith. He would purposely get into trouble, keeping him occupied and getting the attention he sought—good or bad. Between the ages of eight and ten, these were things that Faith did not expect from her adolescent. She felt this was toddler behavior. Nonetheless, Hope was still trying after all those years to get the attention of his Love.

Faith tried to keep him occupied with various activities, but it was impossible for her to be around or keep him occupied 24/7. Eventually, slowly, she allowed Love to re-enter Hope's life with promises of turning over a new leaf and wanting to be the Love that Hope had been craving. He walked the straight and narrow for a while: calling, coming to see him, taking him here or there, and giving him money—all the things that made both Faith and Hope believe this time would be different. That dream was short lived. It was not long before Love's true colors began to shine and Hope's dreams were shattered yet again.

Children Have an Entitlement

We bring kids in this world and feel the joy and pain of their growing up. But what are they entitled to? I thought children were entitled to love and attention from their parents—both parents, whether the parents are together or not.

. . . . *Your child has an entitlement.*

Children are entitled to financial support to ensure they have the necessities of life. There is no choice. That is your responsibility as a parent. Your child did not ask to be conceived; that was your choice. Now you have to pay. But is the payment that severe? Think of the outcome—when your child is able to stand strong and stand tall because of the nutrients and nourishments that came from your hands.

. . . . *Your child has an entitlement.*

Children are entitled to unconditional, emotional affection. Why not? Teach your child how real love is supposed to look and feel. Or is it that YOU do not know what real love is; therefore, you carry an inability to show and teach the same? Well figure it out! That is not your child's burden to bear. Think of all these things before you lay down to unprotected sex.

. . . . *Your child has an entitlement.*

Teach your child the importance of expressing themselves. If you support your child financially but do not show them love, how will they know how to love? How do they grow to know love and respect for a man or woman? How do they know first and foremost how to love and respect THEMSELVES? This is learned and imitated behavior. It is not genetics! Children practice what they see; therefore, parents should practice what they preach. Ohhh—you want them to have respect for you and for others, but you do not want to show them respect. Why? How is that fair? You have to give to get in this 50/50 world that we live in. The relationship with your child is no different.

.... *Your child has an entitlement.*

Children are entitled to physical attention. You MUST be there! How will your children act and respond to situations if they do not see it from you? Do you want them to learn it from someone else? This is your responsibility as parents not theirs as children. Why?

Because your child has an entitlement; and that entitlement is YOU!

—Terryl Ebony

Your First Born

Dad,

I love you to death
Because you and my mom
Gave me breath
I am your first born

We used to have a lot of fun
Now it seems like you are on the run
Are you a father, a daddy or a stranger, man?
Please tell me now because I do not understand.

You were supposed to stick around
And take care of me
Teach me to be a man
Then set me free

But you came and you left
Was I even a thought?
For your first born child
You could've fought

A little harder to keep me near
Hold me close, not stand clear
I need you; I want you in my life
Will you be around to meet my wife?

I used to be angry
Because I felt so torn
I did not understand how a man
Could turn his back on his first born

But now I am growing up and becoming a man
You are missing out on something grand
It makes me sad, just thought you should know
The dad who used to be my idol . . . . is now my foe

—YOUR FIRST BORN

CHAPTER 8:
Losing Love

By the time Hope became a pre-teen, he had already come to a few conclusions about the love of his life. He knew that he would always love him and although he did not respect him, he would never **disrespect** him. He knew that a part of him would keep trying to reach out and connect, knowing that the feeling would not always be reciprocated. He knew that he could not depend—or trust—Love in anyway. His words held the weight of the minute it was said. After that, it was worthless. He knew he had to live and move on and live his life. But how? He continued to search for answers and search for ways to accept the situation as it existed. Faith looked on and offered a listening ear and a shoulder to cry on when needed. She really did not know what else to do or say.

It was senior year of junior high school—one of the happiest times in Hope's life—but how could he be if the Love he wanted was not there to share in the fun. Faith could see the pain in his eyes and hear it in his voice. She tried not to show it in front of him, but her emotions got the best of her when Love called to ask for graduation tickets. "Are you serious?" was her initial reaction. From that point on, all the other words that came out were just words of wrath and fury. She could not believe her ears. The audacity of this man to show up after not calling or coming by for months to see how his son was doing personally or in school, not providing any financial, emotional or physical help—yet still, here he was wanting to take part in one of the most special moments in both a child's and parent's life. He was not even aware that he missed the excitement Hope felt in picking his prom outfit and actually going and having an amazing time. *"Is not there something a father says to his child on prom night?"* she thought. Her son never got those words. All he got was constant neglect from the one person he wanted to impress most in his life.

Faith had had enough of the "revolving door" attitude. She did not understand why he just did not stay away entirely. She was fed up. She thought it would be best for her son not to have his father in his life at all, if this was all he had to offer. So she put her foot down and told him to stay away from Hope. He stayed away before by choice; this time it was by demand.

At that time, Hope had pretty much adapted the "do not care" mentality. On the outside where everyone could see, would be this hard shell filled with a nonchalant attitude that said "Nothing fazes me and I do not care if I get in trouble." He became self-destructive and purposely defiant. Thank God he never turned to drugs or alcohol. He was more of the "I am going to do what I want to do when I want to do it" type of child. This pertained to school work, homework and anything that had to do with being home. He did not want to do chores, clean his room, or help out in any way, shape or form. It was a task at times just to get him to take a bath. Faith began to believe that this problem went far beyond just daddy—son issues. The emotional effects of him not having his father around had somehow equated to a negative home life. Hope did not feel a part of the family because his father was not present. In his eyes, there should be mother, father and child—the complete family unit. The more he thought of it, the more he alienated himself from all the other men in his life. Although he appreciated their help, at the end of the day they were not his Love. He even wondered why they were willing to mentor him and take on certain responsibilities that Love had clearly ignored. It made him leery, untrusting and insecure.

- -

Consistency is vital. Parents, you cannot flip-flop your actions, behaviors, or comments with your children. They are watching, listening and learning from everything you say and do. They learn how to live stable lives based on the foundation you set for them from birth. So if you allow people to come in and out of their lives from a young age, then they will think this is normal behavior and will more than likely emulate these actions as adults.

They also learn how to tell the truth based on your truths. So, if you are consistently breaking promises or going back on your word (even if you feel It is for a good reason), you are teaching them to lie. You must be consistent. The inconsistency will confuse children and they will eventually formulate their own meaning of what is going on and usually their interpretation is a negative one.

- -

For a while Hope tried to speak to his father against his mother's wishes. When she found out, she was not upset with Hope because she understood his actions. However, he knew she would be disappointed and he felt he had to hide and go behind her back. But she also knew she put him between a rock and a hard place, even if it was for his protection. She was definitely upset with Love, mainly for encouraging Hope to be secretive and deceptive. She felt that was disrespectful and unacceptable for a father to teach his child. Should not you teach your children to always tell the truth, regardless of the outcome?

As Faith tried to clean up after the damaging words and actions that Love left behind, Hope was left once again with this feeling of emptiness. He became embittered and angry at both parents for the mess of a life they had created for him. While he was able to verbalize his feelings with Faith, he was unable to do so with Love. Since he knew Love would not understand and because he wanted to salvage what was left of their relationship, Hope kept quiet about his feelings. He just listened or said enough to have the questions stop.

All of the years of tears and broken hearted promises had finally reached their boiling point. All Hope could think of was unleashing his anger on Love with his fists. Faith had stopped him on numerous occasions from approaching Love in that manner. She still felt he should have respect, not necessarily because he was Hope's father but because he was an adult.

So knowing that fighting Love was not an option, he began to fight other children. This was not what Faith had in mind. He claimed fighting would theoretically numb the pain for the moment. Faith was at her wit's end and after speaking to several people she made one of the hardest decisions she would ever have to live with for the rest of her life. She decided to give Hope what he had wanted for so long—an opportunity to spend more time with Love, to get to know him and he wanted Love to know him, too. This was their big break. She sent Hope to live with Love. She felt he was at the age that he could handle the truth about Love's life. He would be able to see Love's lifestyle with his own eyes. For Hope, this was the time for him to prove that he was worthy of his father's attention. Again, he knew he could look to a few others for that father figure influence, but for some reason, the substitutes were just not filling the void he felt. And although the anger he felt toward his Love was still present, he was determined to make the best of it—trying to look at the glass half full instead of half empty.

- -

There are times when parents have to put aside their own personal feelings to do what may be best for their child. Ego, pride and outside forces often prohibit us from doing the best we can for our children. Do not let society, the norm, or your personal baggage cloud your judgment. Take all of that away, look at the bigger picture then make your decision. Usually it will be the right one.

- -

Many people did not think it was a good idea, but Faith felt this was an option that needed to be explored. She knew there would be some backlash but also felt it was an opportunity that a teenage boy needed in order to possibly connect to his father in a way he never had before. She knew the experience could go either way, but it was a risk she was willing to take after feeling as if she had tried everything. She knew, if not anything else, Hope would be able to move on knowing that he tried and that he gave it is all. So with Hope in her heart, Faith sent him to Love. He would no longer be an only child. He would now be in a house with a brother and sisters as he began to get to know them. He was excited and Faith was excited for him. Of course, she missed him terribly, but he was close enough in proximity that she would still get to see him regularly.

Here Hope was in a house that was not his home, surrounded by people he never lived with but had known for years. This was new and unfamiliar territory. He was happy for the opportunity but still upset at that fact that his mother—the one person he always relied on, had gone through great lengths to teach him a valuable lesson. He did not see it as a lesson to be learned. He viewed it more as a punishment and he resented her for it. She understood how he felt, but she could not think of the present; she had to think about his future. What would be best for him in the long run? All the different questions and feelings that lingered within him would now receive answers. That was most important. She could deal with the present animosity knowing his future would be brighter because of it.

Hope was still feeling lost and unwanted but now he felt he had more to prove than he did before and so did Love. Everyone said the new living arrangements would be a bad idea. Both Hope and Love were on a mission to prove them wrong. Deep down inside Faith knew there was some truth to what was being said. But she also knew that there was a lot of good that could come out of it as well. Hope would be exposed to a whole new way of life. There was bound to be good and bad to come out of it. However, their energies were misplaced. They really had nothing to prove to anyone but everything to prove to themselves. They needed each other; they wanted it to work. But, they came across two major obstacles. The first was communication and the second was boundaries.

Hope and Love tap danced around what they wanted to say. No one said how they truly felt. It was more left to the imagination. This created a lot of turmoil, confusion, and frustration. Love was trying to find a place of comfort with his son after many years of distance, while Hope was angry and confused as to why Love could not figure him out. Faith tried to be the mediator, explaining to Love the best way to approach Hope if he really wanted him to open up. She also tried to help Hope understand why Love would not understand him as she did. Her efforts helped to begin the mending process, but they had a long way to go. Little by little the story of Hope's life and his feelings began to unfold. The anger of all the years, from birth to present, began to surface. A war of words was about to take place. Faith encouraged him to speak his mind and get it off his chest. "Do not suppress your feelings to the point of self-destruction. Let it out! Say what is on your mind. Say what is troubling you." Faith knew this would be the best way to heal the wounds and start anew.

Then there were the boundaries. Love felt he could win Hope over by giving him more freedom than he received when he was living with Faith. This won him brownie points with Hope but quickly backfired on him. Hope knew what his father was doing and took full advantage of it. He would stay out later and later. He did not like to do homework before; now he did none at all. He knew Love did not have the time or patience to follow up with teachers like Faith did and took full advantage of it. His grades began to suffer. Faith warned Love about his actions but still gave him the freedom to deal with Hope his way. She knew both of them would have to learn the hard way. Love did not really see the damage that was brewing because he too was raised with a latitude of freedom. He thought this lack of guidance and boundaries was normal.

- -

Very often a parent tends to raise their child based on how that parent was raised. This can have both positive and negative effects. There are a few things that you should keep in mind. First, you must take an honest look at how your life turned out. If you have any doubts or regrets about the actions and decisions that you made, think about the way your parents related to you in that particular area of your life. You will probably find that they were either too disciplined or not disciplined enough and with that honest knowledge you may want to take a different approach to your child's upbringing.

The second thing you want to consider is the generation gap. Every few years the way things are done changes. Parents have to learn to adapt and be flexible to change. If not, you will be raising your child in a current society, based on past times and disciplines, which can lead to disastrous future outcomes. Do not, for one second, assume that your child will handle a present day situation as you did when you were his/her age. Although your child came from you and has many of your features and characteristics, he/she is still his/her own person. That child still thinks and reacts for himself/herself. This is a common fallacy amongst parents.

Lastly, you want to know your child. Every child is different and each child will respond to any given situation in his or her own way. You can have five children living under one roof and they are all unique and will handle situations differently. You cannot base the outcome of one child on the actions of another. If one child excels there are no guarantees that the other child will excel and vice versa.

- -

Hope began to compare the family lifestyle with Faith to where he was now living. In the beginning he tried to camouflage how he was really feeling but as always there was one person he could never hide from—Faith. She could see through the mask and saw his growing depression. In his eyes, things were not going well at all. He liked reconnecting with his siblings before the sibling rivalry began. He felt what it was like **not** to be the only child in the house. He was now living with a large family which opened his eyes to another side of life, some of which were good and some not so good. Still, he had to make the best of it. He began to remember all the things Faith had taught him, the way and the reasons she gave behind her disciplinary actions. He did not get that there and it was confusing. It made him angry because he could not understand his father's parenting style. Although he took advantage of it, it did not sit well with him. He had very little chores, a later curfew with no explanations as to where he would be and had very little to accountability.

As the days went on and Hope started to adjust to his new way of life, new way of thinking and new way of doing things, he also began to lose touch with who he was and all that he wanted to become. He lost focus in school, and his grades suffered tremendously. Hope had hit an all-time academic low, and neither he nor Love knew how he would pull himself out of it.

Faith saw her son perishing before her eyes and although she was hurting, she knew she had to let this play out for as long as she could. When she realized that the semester was coming to an end and not much was being done to rectify the situation, she took control and her maternal instincts surfaced. She had given them both a few weeks to turn the situation around and if it did not, Hope would have to return home. They were not happy with her ultimatum, but they all agreed that it was in Hope's best interest.

By this time, Hope began to see Love for who he really was and although he still wanted his Love, his father, his daddy, he finally realized he could no longer be naïve. Acceptance of one another is something else Faith instilled in him from young. He slowly began to do just that—know and accept Love. He may not like all the things that Love had to offer, but it was now his choice whether or not he wanted to deal with Love. Where Faith had made all the decisions when he was younger, he was now of age where he could provide significant input and she allowed him to do just that.

It was now time to see where Hope was academically and just as Faith had thought, he did not progress enough to stay. Therefore, it was time to say goodbye to the life that brought about a better understanding of Love. The experience of living with Love—his step mother—and siblings was truly a learning one. He may not have liked all that he learned or saw, but most importantly rather than most, he learned who his Love was and came to terms with the fact that he might never change. Love also learned a few valuable lessons along the way. He began to truly understand Hope. It was shocking for Love to see and experience for himself the way Hope thought and viewed life. This was Love's first real lengthy hands on experience with his son. It was amazing to see their similarities and their differences. But Love realized at this point, that they both needed each other. However, Hope's biggest concern was not whether or not he would remain a part of Love's life. It was more, will Love resume his revolving door relationship or will he pick up and enhance what they finally started to create?

To the fathers who want to have a relationship with their child, but just do not have a clue:

Do not be afraid to hug your son, kiss your son, and be sensitive to your son. He is you! Love him like you would like to be loved. It will not stop him from being a typical boy. It will send the right message that it is ok for a man to be compassionate.

However, do not let anyone, including the child's mother, change the positive messages you are teaching your child. She can never love them the way you can and vice versa. A father is irreplaceable.

I grew up without a father and God knows I wish I had someone to look at me the way I look at my son.

—Chetwyn Williams

Side By Side

Dedicated to my mother—Monica Pickering

Mother,

Your presence has impacted my life
You have the gift of touch without using your fingers
The gift of sight without using your eyes
The ability to reach me and give insight where I appear blind
This phenomenon really blows my mind

Where were you when I needed a shoulder to cry on?
Or unleash my fears . . .
Right by my side wiping my tears

When I had dreams and lifelong aspirations
Where were you?
Right by my side with loving inspiration

As I grew older and wondered what life had in store
Where were you?
Right by my side showing me more

Teaching, scolding and dropping little clues
Sometimes even singing the blues

Now that I am older and can appreciate your gift of life
Your gift of touch and
Your gift of sight
I can move on with little fright

In return one day you may need a shoulder to cry on
Or walk a path that brings you fear and
Where will I be?
Right by **your** side wiping **your** tears

—Terryl Ebony

CHAPTER 9:
Having Faith

Some people say that there are three sides to every story: your side, their side, and the truth. Faith has a similar rationale when it comes to matters of the conscience. Her belief is that there is a right and a wrong—period. There is no third reason, excuse, or explanation. She felt people should realize they are either right or wrong for whatever reason and live with the consequences—good or bad.

Those who believe in Faith know that expectations are very high, of her and of others. People should follow one set of rules and not make them up as they go along. That is her belief and that made finding love very easy—but keeping it—would prove to be very difficult. Many men were intimidated by her demeanor and outspoken behavior. She was not good at biting her tongue and she felt honesty was the best policy, which is why she had no problem Telling her son's father when he was slacking off.

Faith is strong and very determined to keep Hope alive. Faith wants Hope to grow up to be resilient and self-reliant. She will always be there to encourage, motivate and empower him to develop and grow into maturity. She knew he would make mistakes and encouraged him to own them and learn from his lessons. She always told him that those experiences would make him a better person. Do not run and hide or be afraid to admit that you messed up. We are all human and mistakes are a part of life.

Regardless of how much faith Hope had, there will never be enough Love. She did not let that deter her goals. Although it would be challenging, she knew her responsibilities. She knew what she wanted and what needed to be done in order to accomplish it. Faith's determination and love for Hope would not let her fail. She did the best she knew how, mistakes and all.

Parents should not be afraid of admitting their mistakes, not even the ones that come with raising a child. No one is perfect. It is okay to make mistakes when you learn from them. Admitting mistakes to your child shows them that you are human and teaches them that perfection is a standard that even the smartest, the coolest or the oldest person cannot achieve.

When Hope was a baby Faith would make sure that he had what he needed to be comfortable: clothes, food, love, attention, education. There was no order tall enough that she would not fulfill. It was actually easy because it was something she wanted to do, something she enjoyed doing for this hopeful baby boy who filled her heart with so much joy. Many people viewed having a child as a job; she viewed it as an honor.

After a while, she realized that she would have to work extra hard because Love was not living up to Hope's expectations. So she had to fill the gap and take up the slack. She made sure he had pleasant memories, as many as she could create. She took pictures every year so he would be able to remember that time in his life; she enrolled him in activities to distract his mind; she connected him with male mentors; she provided family night and family time, trips and events—anything she thought would help him feel secured and loved.

Having personal faith that everything would work itself out is what gave her that extra push. There were many days and nights that she thought she would not be able to pull it off—not live up to the responsibilities of a good parent. There were times when the tears built up and the frustration and emotions took over her rational state. She became enraged over what she believed to be unfair justice. After all, she knew from conception that she would have to fight this battle alone. In the back of her mind, she had lots of hope that Love would turn a new leaf. But she never shared those thoughts with anyone and it never happened. It did not surprise or disappoint her because it was not an expectation; it was a dream—hope for Hope.

- -

Lesson learned . . . Do not be mad when the truth was given to you at the gate and you decided to try to change it. Yes, sometimes that may work, but it is not concrete. You are then setting yourself up for disappointment and aggravation. If it works out, then great! But if it does not, you should not be mad at the other person. You should not even be mad at yourself. Chalk it up to a risk that you took that did not pan out the way you anticipated. And, that is ok. That does not mean give up; it just means you need to accept the hurtful truth.

Accepting the truth can be hurtful, but it is better than a lie. We often put forth unachievable expectations on a person knowing beforehand that that person is not willing and/or capable of meeting those expectations. That is setting someone up for failure. How is that fair to that person? Even if we feel that someone should measure up to our ideals, we cannot force anyone to act selflessly. In terms of parenthood, some people can be coerced to maintain their financial responsibility, but there is no coercion for physical or emotional responsibility. Very often, the physical and emotional obligations are more valuable than the financial duties.

- -

While in school, battling self-esteem issues became a huge issue for Hope. These were the times when Faith would wish there was a man around to provide a different kind of confidence than she had to offer, one coming from a manly place when boys start to become men. But just like all the other growing moments up to this point, Faith had to find the right words. Although there were times when the questions or the situations were bigger than she imagined, she would never let them go unanswered. She would always note the question and ask questions of her own—to other men that is. After taking in all the input received, she would then go back to Hope in her own words, making sure that he had a little more clarity than when the conversation started.

Faith had no problem admitting she did not know. It was how she stayed true to Hope and at the same time taught him that it was okay to ask questions and rely on others for answers. However, it was very important to her that she also taught him to take all the information he received and draw his own conclusion. Have a mind of your own is what she always preached. Do not let people think for you. Let your decisions be yours and then own them, good or bad.

Faith also had the dubious responsibility of teaching acceptance. However, before she could teach acceptance she had to learn it herself. It took many years of hurt, pain, frustration, and tears before she was even open to the idea. Then it took even more years for her to actually know how to accept someone for who they were—as opposed to—the pre-conceived expectations she had set. It was in that moment that Faith realized wrong and right was not as simple as black and white.

She could then take her new lessons and apply them to her son, teaching him that people are known to fail us, but through inner faith and strength you can achieve your goals. That began to be her teaching model—depend and expect nothing from anyone—leaving less room for disappointment. If you get something you want, then consider it a pleasant surprise, but if it does not come you are not disappointed because you were not relying or depending on it.

Because of all her endeavors, Faith began to acquire much of knowledge about parenting. She was now in the presence of many other parents, children and experts in the field. She quickly realized that her model of not expecting anything was also a bit tainted. She quickly rectified what she told her son and apologized for all the years of misguidance. She reassured him it was out of love. She explained that children should have expectations of their parents as parents have expectations of their children.

- -

A good parent is constantly learning and teaching their child(ren). A good parent is open to new possibilities. Children pick up on this positive energy and it rubs off on them. When you see your child making good or bad decisions, you have to take partial credit for it because their decisions are based on concepts that you have taught them either verbally or through your actions. So let the things they see and hear from you be that of a positive nature.

A mother's significance is to create a design to be followed and to implant the perception that a woman is beautiful so he would hopefully understand the need to see the whole as such.

—Onika Pascal

The Man Who Thinks He Can

If you think you are beaten, you are.
If you think you dare not, you don't
If you'd like to win, but think you can't,
It's almost a cinch that you won't.

If you think you'll lose, you're lost,
For out in the world we find
Success begins with a fellow's will;
It's all in the state of mind.

If you think you're outclassed, you are;
You've got to think high to rise.
You've got to be sure of yourself before
You can ever win a prize.

Life's battles don't always go
To the Strongest or fastest man;
But sooner or later the man who wins,
Is the one who thinks he can.

—Walter D. Wintle

CHAPTER 10:
Finding Hope

Hope continued to feel as though he was not good enough. After all he took a backseat to his younger siblings, Love's work, activities, friends, and everything else except the one thing he wanted. He was angry at Love's neglect and just as angry at Faith's protection. He was conflicted because he did not understand Faith's actions. He did not see how other parents could not be the way she was. He realized that a parent giving their child that much freedom was great from a kid's perspective. However, from a parent's perspective it was the wrong thing to do. He often compared his life to the life of his peers. In comparison, he felt caged, trapped like an animal with nowhere to run, nowhere to hide.

Through the years, Love's consistent negative behavior just left Hope with more unanswered questions and added frustrations. He would start off with good intentions but would somehow stray. Faith was also consistent in her behavior. She would always try to shield Hope from the backlash of Love's irrational yet consistent behavior. Her methods were not always to Hope's liking because it came to a point where she also had to make a decision and either way she knew Hope would feel hurt and pain. So she had two choices: allow Love to continue to be a revolving father and see the constant look of hurt and confusion in her son's eyes every time, or remove Love from the picture altogether, eliminating the stop-and-go behavior. Either way this would be a no-win situation for Hope and his behavior showed his displeasure.

Hope's anger and frustration increased by what seemed to be minute by minute. At first glance, he seemed to be fine then you could see his distant look of aggravation. Not knowing how to deal with his anger coupled with idle time, Hope found himself in a lot of trouble. At times, that mischief became very dangerous for him and the people around him.

Hope had a hard time deciphering where or how to take out his anger, where he belonged or if he belonged. He had been disappointed too many times. After a while it got the better of him—fighting, disrupting class, becoming defiant were all signs that he needed more attention. Faith ran out of options and at that point she had tried everything from talking and time outs to grounding to spankings. Nothing seemed to work, and she felt him slipping away until her aunt mentioned counseling. That became her means to an end. But even that worked only for a short time.

Hope began to find solace in his pen. He would write about his feelings. His pad was filled with darkness, loneliness, hurt, sorrow, and pain. There was not much happiness in his writings. Not that there were not happy times; they just did not stick around long enough to be worthy of his words. His words were so gut wrenching and heartbreaking. How could anyone feel this way? Why should anyone have to carry around such a burden, especially a child? At this point, Hope needed something bigger than anything either of his parents could provide. He needed prayer.

- -

Faith is something that all parents need while raising a child. It is not an easy journey, but it can be a fulfilling one. Sometimes we need a little help from a Higher Power. Imagine what your child is going through. Some parents feel as though a child should have no problems because the child does not work and has no bills. Work and bills are actually easy problems compared to self-esteem and peer pressure.

If your child is lost and cannot seem to find his/her way, this is when the child needs you most. Do not view it as a passing phase in life. If the child does not figure it out, then it will not pass; it will linger and haunt them into adulthood. Prayer can be an outlet, a place where your child may be able to find peace. Teach your child to explore it.

- -

Faith did more research and was told about a nearby church that was well known throughout their community. She did not attend much church growing up, so this was new territory. But if there was the slightest possibility that it would save her son, then she was willing to give it a try. She decided to attend one Sunday to see what it was about and what a feeling she got upon entering, during the sermon and while leaving. It was a wonderful feeling and from that day on, she and her son began to go regularly. She insisted that he enlist in Bible study as well. She was trying everything possible.

As each day went by, there was calmness in the air, a brighter spirit, and a sign of hope. The laughter on the outside started to coincide with the happiness on the inside. Hope was starting to learn to love himself despite his surroundings. He began to combine Faith's teachings with that of the Bible along with some advice from his new church brothers and sisters. The combination helped him to learn that he was not responsible for other people's actions but he was responsible for his own.

Change was slowly building for the better. Hope was beginning to understand that he was not responsible for Love's actions, for Faith's actions, or the actions of anyone else that may have disappointed him in the past. This was really the first step toward him "finding" Hope. Faith could definitely see the light at the end of the tunnel. She was finally beginning to see his grades improve and begin to stabilize. He was showing great promise.

Continuing on a journey in the Lord, trying to recognize his identity, and trying to cope with that day to day operation called life, Hope was feeling overwhelmed yet confident. Every day would be a new struggle just to maintain and try to control his anger. It was difficult, but he faced the challenge and as always he had Faith there to encourage him and cheer him on.

Slowly putting down his pen and gravitating more to the computer, Hope started to transform his words and feelings into animation. He started to find comfort in visual arts and decided he wanted to pursue graphic design as his major. Now in high school, he knew he had to step up his game. He also felt there were a lot of expectations, everyone watching and wanting him to achieve the best.

He got off to a great start: a new school, a new journey, new friends, and a whole new take on his life. He was ready! Nothing or no one would stand in his way. Now, he was more determined than ever to finish high school and attend college. His attitude began to change. He seemed to become more and more focused and began to slowly distance himself from the person he longed to be most like. He started to look at life through different eyes, eyes that held promise, eyes with a future, and it did not necessarily include his Love. If he was there, that was great! But if he was not he knew he would still progress and be all that he could be.

Hope reached a point where he did not want to be like his Love, which was a switch from the younger years when he idolized this man, yearned for him, and could not understand why he remained so aloof. Now he cared, but he did not care to the point where it would hinder his progress. He would move forward and continue to dream the big dream until it became a reality. Hope had finally begun to find his identity. He had his own style of dress and personality which came with a new set of friends. They each care for one another. They all encouraged and motivated each other. Hope had finally found a place where he felt he truly belonged. He could be himself without judgment. Prior to high school the only other place he felt that was with Faith.

There were many times where Hope faced criticism from his peers about the way he dressed and many of his beliefs. There were times when their words bothered him but for the most part, Faith encouraged him to continue being and doing whatever felt most comfortable. Taking her advice, he did not change for anyone. He did not compromise his integrity. He believed in friendship and would not allow people to speak negatively about his friends. He would defend their honor without hesitation. This is who he was and who he was proud to be.

He began to change his outlook on life. He began to focus more on how he could channel his anger. As life progressed, he went from writing, to graphics, and then to acting. He sought roles that would keep his audience laughing, but he was just as good in those roles that required deep emotion. So acting became an outlet. Faith supported his decisions but encouraged him to always have a backup plan. He decided that he would pursue both an acting career and one in graphic design. This way he would always be doing something he loved.

Everyone paid attention when Hope opened his mouth to speak. He was very articulate and loved to debate. He had a way of commanding attention and now he had many outlets in which to do it. Hope was a part of many youth organizations, mentoring programs, and other avenues that gave him a voice and a place where he could continue to grow spiritually, artistically, academically, and personally. His schedule was very hectic and Faith realized that he actually functioned better by doing more. He thrived and succeeded under pressure.

Everything seemed to be falling into place for Hope. He was comfortable with his friends, his career choices, his spirit, his Faith and his Love. There was still a way to go, but he was definitely headed in the right direction . . . . finally. He knew to make it all come together he would have to improve his grades in school and he was committed to doing so. He knew that he would have to work hard and he Faith would stay on top of him. College was only two years away and he was going to be ready. No matter the obstacle he was now ready to face it head on because he knew who he was and what he wanted. Hope was finally comfortable in his skin.

- -

A child needs freedom to express himself/herself, to make mistakes and learn from them. This is how the child begins to know who he/she is. If you shelter him/her from all of life's challenges, then he/she will just be a shell of who you want them to be. You must allow him/her to find his/her identity. Yes, it is your responsibility to guide him/her, just remember you cannot live life for him/her. Experiences have got to be your child's own.

- -

Finding Hope

When looking back at all that we endure
The good, the bad, down to the core
We often mistake the challenges we face
As consequences we choose not to embrace

But every road block and stumbling phase
Is a part of life's complicated maze
It strokes us and grooms us to be who we are
From beginning to end, near and far

It is not always easy to figure out
What this thing called life is all about
The trials and tribulations that we must overcome
Is often stressful and never fun

But it is when we succeed that we feel our best
That we rose to the challenge and passed the test
So when you think you are at your lowest peak
Do not give up; this is the time to seek

The courage and strength that we hold within
Coupled with blind faith and love to the end
Will lead you to conquer your deepest fears
While finding hope throughout the years

—*Terryl Ebony*

To the young men constantly seeking their Father, their Daddy, and their Love:

Try to find the closest positive male role model in your life. Ask them to be your mentor. If that is not possible, find your local boys and girls club or its equivalent and sign up for a mentor program. Do not waste time, energy and emotion looking for a dad who is not there and probably will not be there. However, if it is closure that you need, by all means pursue the hunt. But definitely have a positive male influence in your life in the meantime.

My dad has done many bad things to me ever since I was born. He left me in my most crucial time of development. He was never there for me, leaving my mother and me on our own. When he did decide to take care of me, he was only there once in a blue moon. He put me through emotional and physical stress. Everything that he did or did not do started to affect other aspects of my life. I was failing in school and my behavior was really bad. It all went downhill from there. One day he would be there for me and the next he would not. The days turned into weeks and the weeks turned into months. My mother and I just could not take any more. She told me to just let go and that is exactly what I did. Now, I just do not let him get to me. Nothing he does surprises or disappoints me anymore. Before I wanted to see him and now it is "whatever". I honestly do not care.

For every child that is experiencing the same problem I am, the best piece of advice I can offer is to relax—think of all the good things your father has done for you and then think of all the bad. If you are like me and the bad outweighs the good, then you may need to let go too. However, you can increase the relationship with your mother. Focus on the people who are doing positive things in your life. If you are the opposite and the good outweighs the bad, then do what you can to fight for your father with all your heart.

Just remember – if you decide to chase after your father, you must be willing to accept the fact that you may only see him once or twice a month (if that). Know that if you make the conscious decision to pursue the relationship and it does not turn out the way you wanted it to, the only person that you can blame is yourself. I say this because it was your decision to give him another chance knowing that he had a past of not being there for you. And that is fine. Just make sure you review the pros and cons.

Think About It!

D. C. Wilson

About the Author

Ms. Terryl Ebony is a parent, entrepreneur, family and youth activist, life coach, and now, an author. Terryl is the Founder and Executive Director of the non—profit organization, The Misunderstood Youth Development Center (MYDC), where the mission is to help understand, develop, and stimulate the minds of our youth. Terryl is very passionate about helping disadvantaged youth and families become mentally and socially prepared to live in a society that has already classified them as a negative statistic. Through her organization, speaking engagements, and her book, Terryl is prepared to advocate for youth and what they need to become productive and successful leaders in the future.

Terryl is family oriented and enjoys singing, dancing, and writing poetry in her spare time. Her biggest accomplishment to date is raising her son, and sharing in the development of her step-daughter. Parenting is such an important part of who she is; all the trials and tribulations have given her the strength to continue on and share her experiences with others. Although she has accomplished much over a short period of time, Terryl knows that her journey is far from over. She aspires to do much more in her community and around the country.

Edwards Brothers Malloy
Oxnard, CA USA
August 20, 2013